AMERICA'S TEAM
★★★★★★★★★★★★★★★★★★★★★★★★★★

No one gave them a chance. No one
believed they coul[...] the [...]
and go on to win [...]
players believed. [...]
another and said, [...]

Then, on Sunday, [...]
1980, millions of Americans watched
the live telecast. They watched incred-
ulously and with gleeful patriotism
as the most irresistible bunch of
Americans in a long time scored their
final victory in a game that epito-
mized their Olympic adventure.

The come-from-behind United States
hockey team performed the impossible. Amid flag waving, foot stomping
and patriotic singing, the Americans
defeated Finland, 4-2, and won the
gold medal. They won it by coming
from behind with three goals in the
third period.

A nation fell in love with this hockey
team. After the final buzzer sounded,
it was time for a celebration from one
end of the country to the other.

It was Jubilation Sunday.

★★★★★★★★★★★★★★★★★★★★★★★★★★

★★★★★★★★★★★★★★★★

MIRACLE ON ICE

★★★★★★★★★★★★★★★★

BY THE STAFF OF
𝕿𝖍𝖊 𝕹𝖊𝖜 𝖄𝖔𝖗𝖐 𝕿𝖎𝖒𝖊𝖘

GERALD ESKENAZI
RED SMITH
JIM NAUGHTON
STEVEN R. WEISMAN
DUDLEY CLENDININ

WITH AN INTRODUCTION BY
DAVE ANDERSON

BANTAM BOOKS
TORONTO · NEW YORK · LONDON

MIRACLE ON ICE
A Bantam Book / March 1980

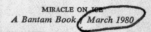

ACKNOWLEDGMENTS:
For THE NEW YORK TIMES: Le Anne Schreiber
Frank Camp, Linda Charlton, Robert M. Klein, Eric Lincoln, Warren Obr and Jed Stevenson.
For TIMES BOOKS: Hugh Howard and Roger Jellinek

Cover photo courtesy of Wide World Photos

Inside cover photos courtesy Duomo Photography

Bantam Books are published by Bantam Books, Inc. Its trademark, consisting of the words "Bantam Books" and the portrayal of a bantam, is Registered in U.S. Patent and Trademark Office and in other countries. Marca Registrada. Bantam Books, Inc., 666 Fifth Avenue, New York, New York 10019.

Contents

★★★★★★★★★★★★★★★★★★★★★★★★★★

INTRODUCTION:
AN OLYMPIC LOVELETTER

★★★★ ★★★★★★★★★★★★★★★★★★★

Dave Anderson

America needed something to cheer about. The hostages in Iran were still in the embassy. Soviet troops were in Afghanistan. Inflation was spiraling. And in Lake Placid, where the XIII Winter Olympics were about to begin, the price of gasoline was soaring toward $1.50 a gallon.

On the snow-muddied streets of the tiny Adirondack Mountain village, the United States hockey players strolled in obscurity. The previous Saturday, at Madison Square Garden, they had lost their final pre-Olympic game, 10–3, to the Soviet Union team. Their coach, Herb Brooks, had shepherded them aboard a chartered bus for the six-hour trip to the Olympic village where they would be lodged in trailers. The Soviet team also had traveled by bus, with one blue-and-yellow New York State Police car in front, another in back; two plainclothes state troopers were on that bus along with what has been described as "the Soviets' own security people," presumably K.G.B. agents.

By any evaluation, the Soviets not only were virtually conceded the Olympic gold medal, but they were considered to be the world's premiere hockey team—the conqueror the previous year of the National Hockey League All-Stars and the best two-of-three Challenge Cup series, including a 6–0 triumph in the decisive game.

The previous Saturday at the Garden, some of the American players had applauded the Russians during the pre-game introductions, an indication of the awe in which they held the Soviet players. To most Americans, the Soviets were faceless—hard, unemotional and mechanical in their red-and-white uniforms and red helmets. But to hockey devotees, the Russians were

1

like gods sculptured in ice, especially Boris Mikhailov, the 35-year-old captain who was about to compete in his fourth Olympics as the Gordie Howe of Gorky Street; Helmut Balderis, the 22-year-old left-wing with the stylish black moustache and the fascinating nickname Elektrichka, meaning The Electric Train; Vasily Vasilev, the 30-year-old defenseman with a slap-shot as loud as gunfire; and Vladislav Tretiak, the lanky 27-year-old goaltender with the spider-like arms and legs.

For all practical purposes, the Russians are professionals. Their occupation is playing hockey. In the Soviet system of state-sponsored sports, they are rewarded with apartments and automobiles far beyond the means of the average workers.

But by Olympic rules, the Russians are amateurs. Ever since the Soviet Union began competing in the Olympics in 1956, it had won every Olympic hockey gold medal except in 1960 at Squaw Valley, Calif., when the United States ambushed the Russians and the Czechs in the medal round. Herb Brooks remembers that team. Then a left wing, he was the last player cut from the American squad.

"The weekend we won the gold medal," he recalls, "I was in St. Paul, drinking beer and watching television."

That year another product of St. Paul, Minn., a goaltender named Jack McCartan, inspired the United States team. He had 39 saves in a 2–1 victory over Canada that catapulted the Americans into the medal round. In a nationally-televised Saturday afternoon game with the Soviet Union, the Americans had fallen behind, 2–1, then Billy Christian, a 5-foot-9-inch forward from the tiny town of Warroad, Minn., near the Canadian border, scored twice, each time on a pass from his brother Roger, for a stunning 3–2 triumph. At the time David Christian was an infant, the son of Billy, the nephew of Roger, at Lake Placid he was a center on this year's Olympic team.

But to win the gold medal in 1960, the Americans

2

had to defeat the Czechs the next morning in a game that started at 8 o'clock. After two periods, the Americans trailed, 4–3.

During the intermission, the Soviet's team captain, Nikolai Sologubov, a balding defenseman, knocked on the door of the Americans' locker room and asked for permission to enter. Once inside, he looked around at the American players and, unable to speak English, gestured that they should take oxygen in order to combat the altitude of the California mountain area. Many of the Americans took his advice. In the third period, the United States rallied for six goals, a 9–4 victory and the gold medal.

Ever since, Olympic idealists have argued that the Soviet captain had suggested the oxygen in the Olympic spirit; others prefer to believe that the Soviets wanted the Americans to win the gold medal, not the rival Czechs.

But two decades ago the Soviets were not a dominant hockey power, they were nowhere near the N.H.L. level.

More significantly, the United States itself was not so aware of the Winter Olympics as it is now. The impact of television has turned the Winter Olympics into a two-week drama that dominates living-room screens. And back in 1960, the American triumph over Canada was considered more of an upset than the victory over the Soviet Union; in those years, hockey was Canada's game.

Although there are several versions of how and when ice hockey began in Canada, the most popular is that the offshoot of field hockey was invented in 1855 by soldiers, the Royal Canadian Rifles, outside their barracks at Kingston, Ontario.

In 1893, Lord Stanley of Preston, Canada's Governor-General, donated the trophy that now is symbolic of the National Hockey League championship— victory in the Stanley Cup playoffs. That same year two Yale tennis players, Malcolm Chace and Arthur Foote, along with Carl Shearer, a Canadian student at

Johns Hopkins University in Baltimore, were credited with importing hockey to the United States. But nearly a century later, the N.H.L. remains dominated by Canadian-reared players.

Only a handful of Americans and Europeans have joined N.H.L. teams; of the Europeans, most have been Swedes who adopted the Soviet style.

As the Olympics were about to begin at Lake Placid this year, the Soviets were the class of the hockey tournament—heads and shoulders and hip pads above every other nation. If any single gold medal was a lock, it was the hockey gold medal that surely would be won by the Soviet team. In other sports, Eric Heiden, the American speed skater, was looked upon as a sure winner of several gold medals—unless he were to pull a hamstring muscle in practice. But for the Soviet hockey team there was no unless, no if.

In the seeding of the Olympic hockey teams, the Soviet Union was rated first, followed by Czechoslovakia, Sweden, Canada, Finland, West Germany and, in seventh place, the United States.

As insulting as that ranking was, it also was understandable. Except for 1960, the United States had never won the hockey gold medal. It had won the silver medal six times—1920 at Antwerp, 1924 at Chamonix, 1932 at Lake Placid, 1952 at Oslo, 1956 at Cortina d'Ampezzo and 1972 at Sapporo—but in 1976 at Innsbruck, it had finished a weak fourth, winning only two of five games, allowing 21 goals while scoring only 15 goals, inlcuding a 6–2 loss to the Soviet Union in the opener. In the 1979 world championship tournament at Moscow, the Americans had finished fifth with a record of two victories, two defeats and two ties.

In forming this year's Olympic team, Herb Brooks decided to use mostly young collegians, including several of his University of Minnesota players. But despite a 60-game training schedule, the team arrived

4

at Lake Placid untested and unknown at the international level.

At this year's Olympic tournament, the Americans were in the Blue Division with Czechoslovakia, Sweden, West Germany, Rumania and Norway.

Almost poetically, if not politically, the Red Division featured the Soviet Union along with Canada, Finland, the Netherlands, Poland and Japan.

Originally, the Olympic tournament was scheduled to begin on Thursday, February 14, but when the Netherlands and Japan were added, the round-robin schedule in each division created an extra game for each team. As a result, the opening of the tournament was moved back to Tuesday, February 12—the day before the pageantry of the Opening Ceremony at the Lake Placid horse show grounds. By the time the American hockey team marched with the other United States Olympians in their red, white and blue jackets, beige cowboy hats and blue jeans, they had already played their first game—a 2–2 tie with Sweden on a last-minute goal by Bill Baker, a 23-year-old defenseman who had played for Herb Brooks at the University of Minnesota.

In retrospect, Baker's goal kept the Olympic torch burning for the American team. Had the United States lost that opener, the players might have been tempted to stop dreaming about a silver medal or a bronze medal. Even in the American players' minds, the gold medal would be won by the Soviets.

But after having salvaged that tie with Sweden, the Americans pounced on the Czechs, 7–3, on Thursday night. To television viewers all over the nation, they now were America's Team, the Olympic dream. The next morning Eric Heiden would win his first speed-skating gold medal in a 500-meter duel in the sun with Evgeny Kulikov of the Soviet Union; on Saturday morning he would win his second gold medal at 5,000 meters. But that afternoon the United States hockey team, trailing Norway by a goal after one period, stormed back for a 5–1 triumph and suddenly the nation was aware of another Madison, Wisc., skater—Mark Johnson, a 22-year-old center who had played peewee hockey with Eric Heiden.

In their next game, on Monday night, February 18, the Americans ripped Rumania, 7–2, and on Wednesday night they got by West Germany, 4–2, to complete the divisional competition with a record with four victories and one tie, the same as Sweden's record. But because of a goals differential, Sweden was awarded first place.

In the crossover scheduling for the medal round, the United States would oppose the Red Division winner, the mighty Soviet Union team, starting at 5 o'clock on Friday afternoon, followed by the Sweden-Finland game.

When the Americans shocked the Russians, 4–3, as goaltender Jim Craig made 36 saves, the nation had something to celebrate, something to restore national pride although the gold medal was not yet assured. But three hours later, Finland simplified the situation by rallying to tie Sweden, 3–3; this meant that the United States would win the gold medal if it defeated Finland in a Sunday morning game, starting at 11 o'clock. By then, Eric Heiden had swept all five gold medals in men's speed-skating, and his sister Beth had taken a bronze. Another speed-skater, Leah Mueller, had won two silver medals and Phil Mahre had won a silver medal in the men's slalom. But nobody in America had anticipated the hockey gold medal. And with the gold medal at stake, the Americans fell behind again, first by 1–0 and then by 2–1, but three goals in the final period produced a 4–2 triumph that ignited a national celebration.

America had something to cheer about.

★★★★★★★★★★★★★★★ ★★★★★★★★★★
PROLOGUE:
THE RUSSIANS ROMP
★★★★ ★★★★★★★★★★★★★★★ ★★★★★
Jim Naughton

Herb Brooks was worried that his United States Olympic hockey team was too confident. "We might need a good kicking to bring us down to earth," he said. The next day, at Madison Square Garden, they got that kicking.

The Soviet Union's Olympic team pounded the United States Olympians, 10–3, and dominated every aspect of the game. The Soviet team, an odds-on favorite to win the gold medal at Lake Placid, got three goals from Vladimir Krutov and outshot the Americans by 35–20. The Russians jumped out to a 4–0 lead in the first period on an array of goals that ranged from workmanlike to spectacular.

The United States team, on the other hand, seemed disorganized and outclassed. Brooks said that was his fault. "I gave them a bad plan," Brooks said. "We should have attacked them." Instead, the American team tried to play a close checking game, which is not its forte. The Americans did hit the Russians, but they went out of their way to do it. "It was senseless," Brooks said, "it was not very smart."

The Soviet coach, Viktor Tikhonov, was also puzzled by the Americans' tactics. "We've got the feeling they have a lot in reserve," he said. Tikhonov thought Brooks would use different tactics if the two teams met in the Olympics.

"I think both coaches took this game as a practice game," Tikhonov said. "Today we showed what we could do but they did not." His words proved to be prophetic.

The Garden had been concerned that there might be anti-Soviet actions by spectators, but there were no incidents during the game, played before a crowd of 11,241 and thousands of empty seats.

The Soviet team began its display early. Two minutes into the game, it held the Americans without a shot on a power play. As soon as the penalty had elapsed, Helmut Balderis slid a pass from the corner to Aleksandr Maltsev, who was alone in front of the net. Maltsev snapped the puck past Jim Craig at 4 minutes 23 seconds. The barrage had begun.

Craig, who was lifted for Steve Janaszak midway through the second period, allowed four goals, three of which he could do little about. The Russians continually broke behind the American defense.

Krutov scored twice within five mintues. His second goal came when he faked Bill Baker, a defenseman, at the line, deked Craig three times and backhanded the puck into the short side of the net.

There were other examples of Soviet dominance in the second and third periods. Boris Mikhailov scored on a textbook power-play goal late in the second period. He skated behind the net, took a pass from Vladimir Petrov on the far point and jammed the puck in the short side before Janaszak could move. That made the score 6–1.

Maltsev scored the most spectacular goal of the game halfway through the third period. He broke in on right wing, deked one defenseman, continued skating toward the net but turned in a complete circle at the same time, and finally snapped a backhand between Janaszak's leg and the near post.

"We learned some things today conceptually," Brooks said of the Soviet display.

However, the lessons were not learned quickly enough to make the outcome respectable. Mike Eruzione got the Americans' first goal, at 17:09 of the second period, but by that time the score was 5–0. Phil Verchota and Steve Christoff scored third-period goals for the United States.

Despite the shellacking, Brooks seemed undisturbed. "Everybody looks like they are going to a wake," he told a group of reporters who gathered around him after the game. "Sometimes a good kicking is good for a quality athlete and a quality team. We won't be demoralized."

8

★★★★★★★★★★★★★★ ★★★★★★★★★★
1: ICEMAN ON A HOT SPOT
★★★★★★★★★ ★★★★★★★★★★★★★★
Jim Naughton

If there were more people like Herb Brooks, perhaps he would not have found himself in such an
uncomfortable position. Brooks, the coach of the United States Olympic hockey team, was in the middle of
what could have become a political event when his
team faced the Soviet team.

Ticket sales for the exhibition event were way off
and the crowd was predicted to be under 10,000, less
than two-thirds capacity. It was a misguided means of
punishing the Russians, as profits from the game go to
the United States team.

There were also those who were afraid of what
those 10,000 might do. The Garden had received several requests to cancel the event, and a spokesman said
the Garden had asked for "a lot of input from a lot of
different protection agencies." He added that all pack-
ages brought into the building would be searched.

In the midst of this tension was Herb Brooks, an
apostle of a low-key approach to just about everything,
a man who just might have been the best person to
handle it. "We don't want an ugly scene," he said. "It
would show the world that we are an insecure people."

In the hawkish profession of coaching, Brooks is
a dove. He is eloquent in a quiet way, determined but
not fanatic. Brooks is ambitious and would like to
coach in the National Hockey League, but he is an-
noyed by people who think winning is an amateur
coach's overriding concern. When asked about the
United States team's chances for an Olympic gold
medal he said, "Slim and none." He said he would not
be disappointed if the team finished fifth or sixth as
long as it played well.

For a man who has built his life around sports he

9

has a refreshing perspective. "I believe an athlete is an insignificant person in view of the world situation," he said.

"I tell my players you should understand the world around you. You should understand the lessons of history."

The lesson of history in regard to Soviet-American hockey games is that the Russians almost always win. That did not bother Brooks; in fact, he said, if the Soviet team won that day, he would not be too upset.

"The Russians have to be good hockey players to lead a good life," he said before the game. "They are hungrier than we are. They are doing everything in their power to show that their way of life is a good way of life, and they are doing it through the vehicle of a sports team. We don't have to do that."

In Brooks's eyes that sort of pressure is what distorts and corrupts a sport. He is bothered by those who are obsessed with victory, whether the roots of those obsessions are nationalistic or commercial. "I don't know if a young man should be bought, sold, fined and suspended when he's between 15 and 20 years old," he said.

Brooks, head coach at the University of Minnesota, might find this approach a bit uncomfortable in the N.H.L., where coaches are fond of making noise about discipline.

What Brooks had done with the young men on the Olympic team was teach them a new style of hockey that emphasizes speed, sharp passing and puck control. It was a radical departure from the dump-and-chase style that is taught throughout most of the United States and Canada. "We take the wraps off our people and let them be creative and innovative," Brooks said.

It was not easy, and had not been completely successful. "They make mistakes," Brooks said, "but they make them with enthusiasm." He compared the team to the little girl in the nursery rhyme: "When we are good we are very, very good, but when we are bad we are horrid."

10

If his team were very good in Lake Placid, Brooks said he thought it might win a bronze medal. But he said he felt that the team had accomplished more than that already. The United States Olympic team was primarily composed of college students. Ten of the 20 players on the team had college eligibility left when the games were over. Sixteen of the 20 had been drafted by N.H.L. teams. A few of them might even be in the Stanley Cup playoffs in the spring of 1980.

In a sport where Americans, especially American collegiate players, are still fighting for recognition, it is odd that so many of them have been drafted by the N.H.L. It was a credit to Brooks and the team that they had done so well, compiling a 42–15–3 won-lost-tied record in their preparation schedule. "I think we have paved the way for future college players to be looked at through different eyes," Brooks said.

Even before the Olympic win, professional teams were starting to look with great interest at Brooks. He had been contacted by "four or five teams" and had "superficial talks" with some. "I would like to coach in the N.H.L.," he said, but would not say when or with whom. He was planning to return to the University of Minnesota in March.

In a way Brooks did not want March to come. The Olympic team had been together for six months, and the players had become close. Brooks gave them an opportunity to grow as players and as people, and they responded. "It's a dream come true for these athletes," he said. "For the first time in their lives they have been able to be with people from different walks of life. I think they've grown."

One almost hopes that Herb Brooks will never become a professional coach because what he is doing now seems more important.

But Herb Brooks said he thought he had some growing to do. It will not be easy, he said, but there will be advantages to having the Olympics end. "I don't want it to end," he said, "they don't want it to end. My wife does."

★★★★ ★★★★★★★★ ★★★★★★★★★

2: THE UPHILL CLIMB BEGINS

★★★★ ★★★★ ★★★ ★★★★★★★★★★★★

Gerald Eskenazi

In a game in which the innovative United States team became the first one in Olympic hockey history to use a spotter with a walkie-talkie conveying information from the stands to the bench, an old-fashioned slap shot proved to be the difference.

The shot was drilled home with only 27 seconds to play by Bill Baker of the University of Minnesota, in front of a crowd of 4,000 that half-filled the new field house as competition opened in the XIII Olympic Winter Games. Baker's 55-footer came with six American skaters on the ice, against five for Sweden, after the removal of the United States goalie, and lifted the underdog Americans to a 2–2 tie against Sweden.

Part of the reason the Americans got this important point in the standing could probably be attributed to the two-way setup between Lou Vairo, a former roller-hockey player from the sidewalks of Brooklyn, who was in the stands, and Craig Patrick, the assistant coach, who was on the bench near Coach Herb Brooks.

The game was critical for the Americans. Under the round-robin system, they play the five other teams in their division, with the top two in each division meeting for the gold, silver and bronze.

The favorite in the other division, the Soviet Union, was greeted with polite applause by the 500 fans who remained in the arena after the U.S. game in the first appearance by a Soviet team in this year's Olympics. But if any controversy affected the Russians it was well hidden. They had an 8–0 lead on 28 shots after the first period against Japan and went on to a 16–0 victory.

But Brooks was not thinking about the Russians.

12

He estimated that America's next opponent, Czechoslovakia, promised to be tough. Czechoslovakia won its opener earlier that day 11–0 over Norway.

Before pulling out the tie, Brooks's team had reverted to some of its American ways against the swift, clever Swedes, who jokingly contend that this is their "B" team. The "A" team, they say, is playing in the National Hockey League.

"Because of our age and lack of experience, the players will revert," Brooks admitted. Still, he said, "Hey, we're happy."

Small wonder. There were long stretches when the United States forgot the intriguing style that Brooks had installed when he created this team last September. The Americans rarely moved with purpose when they did not have the puck, a key element in Brooks's synthesis of the old and the new. Instead, they remembered only to play the body, slamming Swedes into the boards and corners.

Brooks had told his players that the Swedes' resolve could wither if they did not jump to an early lead. But they did.

There is no mistaking the skill of the Swedish team. Although almost 5 percent of the N.H.L.'s 400 players are Swedish, their Olympic team remains a solid one. The Swedes scare opponents with one particular play: in bringing out the puck, their center spins near the blue line luring a defender. At the same moment, a wing performs the same maneuver, and suddenly there are two whirling Swedes, and confusion over who covers them.

Yet it was a traditional-type goal that gave Sweden an early lead. Although Jim Craig, the Boston University goalie, had performed spectacularly with the stand-up style that Brooks demands against Europeans, he was helpless when Sture Anderson got in front and simply swiped home a centering pass.

The Americans did not match the goal until only 28 seconds remained in the second period, putting enormous pressure on Pelle Lindbergh, the 20-year-old Swedish goalie, and winding up with a score by Dave Silk, Craig's college teammate.

Still it appeared that the walkie-talkie advice from Vairo had been wasted when Thomas Eriksson gave the Swedes a 2–1 edge in the final period—there are no overtimes in Olympic play.

The last time that Vairo had tried to use a walkie-talkie in a game was some years ago at Coney Island—and he was suspended by the commissioner of the Brooklyn Juniors League, where he coached.

Vairo contended that using it in the game with the Swedes was legal. In the opening minutes of the game, for example, he advised Patrick by walkie-talkie, "they're going with four lines."

"O.K., thanks, I'll tell the coach," replied Patrick.

Brooks made some important adjustments, for the four Swedish lines were trying to exploit the Americans' lack of depth. Fresh Swedish players were always covering Mark Johnson, the University of Wisconsin star. Other fresh Swedes were continually storming through. It was Craig in the goal who provided the difference.

Whatever the goalie's thoughts were later, he was not permitted by Brooks to disclose them. Brooks would not permit his American players to be interviewed in the first Olympics to be held in the United States in 20 years.

Brooks, who has been asked by Fred Shero to join the New York Rangers organization, can be hard on his players. He even refused to discuss what he had told his players between periods.

★★★★ ★★★★★ ★★★★★★★★★★ ★★★★
3: "LET THE PRESSURE FALL ON ME"
★★★★★★★★★★★★★★★★★ ★★★★★★★
Gerald Eskenazi

Jim Craig of Boston University said he knew that he would be the calmest American on the ice in the next game. He also said he knew that he must stop the powerful Czechoslovak team.

The American hockey team was expected to teeter on a fine edge of tension. Its coach, Herb Brooks, is a motivator of young men, and at the University of Minnesota he has compiled one of the most successful collegiate records.

But he also is a screamer, and while the low-keyed Craig refused after the game with Sweden to talk about the Brooks style, he said a lot about it with this comment: "Some things are better left unsaid. You never second-guess a guy."

Whatever happened, the Americans at that moment were in the middle of the pack on the road to a medal. Under Olympic rules the top two finishers in each of the two six-team divisions meet for the three medals. Brooks knew his two toughest games in the first phase of competition would be against the Swedes and the Czechoslovaks. A pair of early losses, he feared, would virtually eliminate the United States.

Now the Americans had some breathing room because if teams are tied after their five-game opening round-robin, then the team with the greater margin between goals for and goals against advances. If they are still tied, the team with more goals scored moves on.

That was one reason why the Czechoslovaks piled it on with an 11–0 victory over Norway, and the Soviet team was merciless, and very physical, in its 16–0 trouncing of Japan. That outcome is not an Olympic record, however. In 1948, the United States routed the Italians 31–1.

Craig said he believed this United States team had an intangible edge over the Europeans: emotion. "Look, the Czechs, the Swedes, they're pros," the goalie said. "They get behind by two or three goals, they just keep skating with you. The same level of intensity. They're getting paid anyway. They don't turn it on in bursts like we can."

Such a spurt gave the United States the tie with 27 seconds to play against the Swedes. When Bill Baker's slap shot sailed home, Craig was on the bench, having been removed for a sixth skater. He did not react to the goal, even after returning to the net for the final seconds. That was how he had trained himself.

"Sure, I wanted to hug Bill," he admitted. "But I couldn't. What would happen if I relaxed and they scored with 20 seconds left?"

Craig was extremely conscious of his role as anchor on the team. This is the first top-level international competition for every player on the team, virtually all of whom were in college last year.

For some, the emotion can work positively. Jack O'Callahan suffered such a severe thigh bruise in the opening period of a game with Sweden that he was not expected to return. But between periods in the locker room he said, "What the hell, to come all this way and not make it because of a bruise in the thigh . . ." And he played.

Craig said he anticipated a similar game against the Czechoslovaks, a team that also plays with an even, unemotional flow.

"They'll get a lot of good shots, 20 to 40 feet out, and I'll have to stop them. I'll have to watch the angles."

The Czechoslovaks' stick work is exquisite, and they also exploit their use of the "offwing"—a right-handed shooter, for example, will play the left wing. This gives him more net to shoot for because his stick is closer to the center of the ice. In this situation, the goalie must remain on his feet more often. Craig said

16

he knew he would have to stand up early in the game.

"I try to make my team feel at ease," the 22-year-old goaltender from North Easton, Mass., said. "I know I must stop the Czechs in the first five minutes. That's O.K., let the pressure fall on me. At least it won't be on my teammates."

For Craig, the most pressure he has ever faced was as Boston University's goalie. "They had a winning tradition there," he explained, "and if you didn't do well, they told you there was always someone who could take your place."

Brooks did not have the luxury of depth, not the way the Swedes, the Czechoslovaks and the Russians did. That was why Craig believed he could not give up more than three goals a game. "Then anything can happen for us, like it did last night," he said after the tie with Sweden.

After the Olympics, Craig and his representatives will talk to the Atlanta Flames of the National Hockey League, who drafted him in the fourth round. But during the games he was happy as an Olympic goalie.

"Yeah," he said. "I worked hard for it. You get what you deserve."

★★★★★★★★★★★★★★★★★★★★★★★★

4: THE FIRST BIG VICTORY

★★★★★★★★★★★★★★★★★★★★★★★★

Gerald Eskenazi

Few would have dared to predict it. But despite the odds, the unexpected happened.

With a buzzing style of play that brought standing ovations throughout the game, the United States hockey team achieved its second straight upset in the XIII Olympic Winter Games, defeating Czechoslovakia, 7–3. In the seedings for the hockey tournament, the more experienced Czechoslovaks were rated second only to the powerful Soviet team, while the United States had been ranked no better than seventh among the 12 teams.

But the Americans' coach, Herb Brooks, said he determined to exploit what he termed his team's "youthfulness, from which comes hungriness." That hunger paid off in the game with the Czechs.

In the opener of the hockey series, the underdog Americans tied the third-ranked Swedes, 2–2, in the last half-minute of the game. With the victory over the Czechs and three games remaining in the five-game preliminary round, the Americans found themselves in a commanding position to advance to the four-team final round.

At this point, with a victory and a tie apiece, the United States and Sweden were tied for first place in their division, while the Russians and Canadians led the other one. In the last 20 years, since they won the gold medal at Squaw Valley, Calif., the Americans had won only one medal in hockey.

But few teams have been motivated and disciplined the way Brooks, a 42-year-old from St. Paul, had done it to this team. His players produced a sparkling game against the Czechs, bringing repeated ovations and flag-waving and chants of "U.S.A." from the first blatantly partisan fans in the new field house.

18

The United States' games under Brooks had been models of clean, aggressive play, but toward the end in this game some of the players retaliated after their most accomplished player, Mark Johnson of the University of Wisconsin, was speared in the shoulder by Jan Neliba. When Johnson, who played high-school hockey with Eric Heiden, the star of the American speed skating team, was speared, Brooks started to scream. His words were picked up over national television by ABC-TV.

"My 72-year-old mother was watching," said Brooks later, smiling. "My poor mother heard that."

But she and a worldwide audience also saw some remarkable hockey, the sort of nonstop, spirited play that Brooks substituted for depth in skill and experience on the American team, which, averaging 22 years, was one of the youngest in Olympic history.

Against the Czechs, the Americans got to the puck faster, their sticks and their pace quicker. And it all confused the Czechoslovaks, who are noted for the craftiness and their ability to take immediate advantage of an opponent's mistakes.

It was that way almost from the beginning, despite the Czechoslovaks' early 1–0 lead. As the game wore along a fresh American line would go out, play its 90 seconds, and come off to a crescendo of applause by fans who paid up to $30 a ticket.

It was like watching performers doing star turns, instead of seeing a group of virtual unknowns in American sports holding center stage in the world arena.

The Americans were to continue their odyssey when they faced Norway, which has been beaten by Czechoslovakia, 11–0, and by West Germany, 10–4. After that, the Americans were to face the Rumanians and West Germans, with the prospect of making it to the final four if they were not upset. The situation was changing dramatically from the first days of the Olympics when the lightly regarded Americans were almost counted out before taking the ice. The United States concentrated on the immediate business in its game with Czechoslovakia, though, after Jaroslav Pouzar smacked a wrist shot past Jim Craig, who believes that if he can hold the opposition to three goals or less, than "anything can happen."

It did. The United States quickly retaliated when Craig's college teammate, Mike Eruzione, scooted down the left side and snapped home a goal. Then followed a score from Mark Pavelich of Minnesota-Duluth, who shoveled in a close shot, and it was 2–1 for the United States.

Before the first period ended, two of the Czechoslovaks' line of the Stastny (pronounced STASH-nee) brothers collaborated. Peter, the center, gave the puck to Marian, the right wing, for the goal and a 2–2 tie. Anton, the left wing, was merely a spectator.

But the Americans took a lead they never relinquished in the second period, on the first of two goals by Buzz Schneider. Johnson put in a backhander later in the session. In the finale, Phil Verchota, Schneider and Rob McClanahan scored, offsetting Jiri Novak's goal.

In hockey, fans like to talk about the number of shots on goal. In this game, that statistic was misleading, for the United States's play was so efficient that they needed only 27 shots at Kralik, the goalie.

In the opener against the Swedes, they showed their nervousness by taking inaccurate but booming slap shots from 60 feet out. The Americans waited this time, moving closer and closer with the puck and gaining confidence as they discovered that, indeed, they could zero in against the Czechoslovaks.

And in the eyes of America, the race for the gold was truly on.

★★★★★★★★★★★★★★★★★★★★★★★★
5: HOW FAR CAN THEY GO?
★★★★★★★★★★★★★★★★★★★★★★★★
Dave Anderson

For at least a fleeting moment, America's team was no longer the Dallas Cowboys, if indeed it ever really was. America's team had become the United States Olympic hockey team.

When the American players, in their red, white and blue uniforms, skated onto the ice at the XIII Olympic Winter Games, spectators chanted, "U.S.A." Some waved American flags, large and small. Banners implored "U.S.A. All The Way," meaning the gold medal. And television viewers all over America, many of whom had thought a hockey puck was an insult in a Don Rickles monologue, were suddenly paying attention to these young Olympians.

In hockey, miracles usually happen because of two factors—home ice and a work ethic. America's team has both. After his squad tied Sweden, 2–2, in its opener on a last-minute goal, Herb Brooks was talking about the work ethic.

"If you want to play this game effectively," the coach said, "you'd better report with a hard hat and a lunch pail. If not, you better go watch some old guys ice fishing."

America's team had another element that often creates miracles. The players were not expected to win, whereas the Soviet players were. In their last pre-Olympic game, the United States squad lost to the Soviet team, 10–3, at Madison Square Garden, but Herb Brooks said he believed that his players "needed a good kicking to wake them up."

Ken Morrow, the bearded defenseman from Davison, Mich., had another positive thought in reflecting on that defeat.

"We considered it the last game of our training. If we got beat, so what?" the 24-year-old player said.

"We had been playing semipro and college and minor-league teams, and when we played the Russians, we were still skating at the same pace in the first period. But by the end of the game, we we were skating at the pace we need here."

Ken Morrow's beard also told something about Herb Brooks, who had a no-beard rule until Ken Morrow showed up with one. "But if I stuck to the rule," the coach said, "he'd be with the New York Islanders now instead of with us, so I let him keep it. I didn't know how else to handle it."

Morrow, along with 12 of his teammates, has been drafted by various N.H.L. teams. Perhaps the best prospect is Mark Johnson, the 22-year-old center from Madison, Wis., who played peewee hockey with Eric Heiden, the winner of five gold medals for speed skating.

"Mark Johnson makes our team go," Herb Brooks said. "We like him to be on the ice 30 to 40 percent of the time."

Mark Johnson's father, Bob, coached the United States team that finished fourth in the 1976 Olympics at Innsbruck.

"That year Mark didn't even go to the Olympics as a spectator," his mother recalled. "He had two important high school hockey games to play, so he stayed home. I think it's just as well because these are the first Olympics he's seen. The first are always the best."

"But they really never talked to me that much about it," David Christian said of his uncle and father and the 1960 Olympic hockey team. "My father's gold medal is on an end table in the living room and I've looked at scrapbooks. But my father and my uncle, who lives next door to us, just aren't the type to talk about something like that. It's something they did, they're proud of it, and that's it."

Warroad, Minn., only six miles from the Canadian border, is known as "Hockey Town, U.S.A."

"The thing is to do there is play hockey," David

Christian said. "The rink, the Warroad Memorial Arena, is open every day from November to April and you don't have to pay to use it. My father still plays senior hockey."

Bill Christian, in Lake Placid for the Olympics, is now 42 years old the Gordie Howe of Warroad, Minn.

"The Warroad Lakers, that's our team," Bill Christian said. "We're going to play in the Allen Cup in Canada this year. But mostly, my brother and I manufacture hockey sticks—700,000 a year."

Bill Christian might not talk much about the '60 Olympics, but he remembered that miracle.

"We beat Canada early, then we upset the Russians, 3–2, on Saturday afternoon and had to play the Czechs the next morning at 8 o'clock for the gold medal. We won, 9–4, but after two periods were were losing, 4–3, when Nikolai Sologubov came into our dressing room and suggested that we use oxygen."

While some idealists thought the Soviet captain was doing that year's American team a favor in the Olympic spirit, realists have always believed that the Soviet players simply did not want the rival Czechoslovaks to win the gold medal. Whatever, the Russians were not likely to help America's team work a miracle this year.

Gerald Eskenazi

The United States hockey team, which was supposed to be virtually eliminated by now, had instead become the most talked-about team of the Olympic Games, where sometimes dreams really do come true.

Following their exuberant and swarming 7–3 upset victory over Czechoslovakia, the Americans were not only tied with Sweden for first place in their division, but they were also television celebrities of sorts, having triumphed in an internationally televised game.

In an era when North American hockey has been in decline and labeled as animalistic by some Europeans, an American team had appeared suddenly that

23

played nonstop, clean hockey. And it was doing it well. The Americans were to face Norway next, and for the first time in three games they would not be the underdogs. They were not expected to stay with the Swedes in the opening game, but they tied them in the last 27 seconds. They were not supposed to be in the class of the Czechoslovaks, but they beat them thoroughly, turning an experienced, physically stronger squad into one that was stunned by thudding body checks and opportunistic American sticks that poked away the puck.

Mike Ramsey of the University of Minnesota—the only American ever drafted by a National Hockey League team on the first round—appreciated what his team had done, and what remained. "If we lose to Norway tomorrow, we'll remember it the rest of our lives," he said.

Many fans will remember the game against the Czechs. It had the drama, fan support and emotion that can be the best part of the Games.

For Ramsey, this is how it was:

"We wanted to win so bad. The feeling in the locker room was unbelievable. It's an emotional high, to think you can stay so high for 60 minutes is unbelievable. We just upset the Czechs."

The victory put the Americans in a strong position to get into the final medal round, which pits the top two teams in two six-team divisions against each other. The United States had already played the toughest teams in its six-team division. The Czechoslovaks and Swedes still faced each other in the round-robin play.

But to get to this stage the Americans had to get past the Czechs. Just before that game, Coach Herb Brooks decided to change his strategy. He was going to exploit his team's youth.

"Go out and use your youth," he told them. "Use your enthusiasm."

They did. Suddenly, they were unafraid to make the extra fake against a defender. They had confidence that they could keep the puck. They zeroed in on the goalie, Jiri Kralik. They took good percentage shots instead of impressive, but wasteful, 60-foot slap shots.

The key to halting the clever Europeans is pressure: keep them from snaring the puck by checking them, or by keeping it yourself. On the fly, they are difficult to stop. Indeed, at game's end one of the Czechoslovak defenders stopped Mark Johnson, the most accomplished forward, by spearing him in the shoulder and sending him crashing to the ice. But Johnson worked out the next day, although his status remained uncertain for the Norway game.

If that game went well for the United States, Brooks probably would keep Johnson on the bench. Ramsey, who has been drafted by the Buffalo Sabres and will be their defenseman one day, contended, "I think that everybody's worried about Norway. We played them in Oslo last fall and tied them, 3–3."

This was hardly the same United States team, though. When Ramsey looked at the schedule that his team was about to undergo, he was stunned: 60 games, with 48 on the road.

Now, for a change, they were the home team.

"I couldn't tell you this before," Brooks said early the morning after the big victory, "but I told my guys that we cannot stand in awe."

6: ANOTHER COMEBACK

Gerald Eskenazi

Suddenly, the United States Olympic hockey team was expected to win. In a boutique arena where Sonja Henie once won a gold medal, 1,400 fans refused to leave, preferring to revel in the afterglow of what they had come to the arena to enjoy: a victory.

The U.S. over Norway by a score of 5–1 guaranteed that the team would remain at least tied for first in the Blue Division with Sweden, which played later the same day against West Germany.

But it was not quite the same Ameriacn team that had moved to the top with a tie with Sweden and an upset victory over Czechoslovakia. Before the game Coach Herb Brooks wondered if he could keep his players' intensity up. "I'm afraid of American kids," he said. "They get too cocky."

While they played with the same quickness they had displayed against Sweden and Czechoslovakia, there was an element of intelligence missing. Early on, the Americans failed to complete their plays, with passes that were just too short, or sticks that were too late on the ice.

Still, it appeared that Norway entered this game determined not to be embarrassed. After all, it had yielded 21 goals in being routed by the Czechoslovaks and West Germans.

So the Norwegians stormed after whomever had the puck for the Americans. They left open patches of ice that could have been disastrous but which the Americans did not capitalize on. They also played the body, often sending Americans into the boards and jarring the spectators, who were so close it must have seemed as if someone was falling down in their living room.

The game was staged in the Olympic arena, the

1932 Olympic arena. Tickets were so scarce that out-side the building it appeared to be a Sunday night at Madison Square Garden at playoff time.

"Who's got tickets? Who's selling?" people shouted. This time there were matrons and children doing the buying, too. The empty seats at Madison Square Garden barely a week before were forgotten.

Inside, the building sparkled. It has been refur-bished, painted bright white and outfitted with new red plastic seats. Because there were so many games in the two divisions, each team had to play at least one game in the old place instead of at the New Olympic Field House.

There was something old-fashioned about the way the Americans played in the early part of the game. Their playmaking was only sporadic and they also had problems with the Norwegian goalie, Jim Marthinsen, who stood up and faced the American shots. Later, perhaps out of weariness or nervousness, he began to flop, to anticipate where the Americans shots would be heading, and he was beaten repeatedly.

His early work prevented a rout. Virtually no one was cheering for him or his teammates The fans included Terry Bradshaw and Jo Jo Starbuck; Charles Tickner, the American men's figure skating champion, and Dianne Holum, coach of the American speed skating team.

Marthinsen kept his head, and the underdog Nor-wegians actually had a 1–0 lead after the first period. It took them more than four minutes to get their first shot because of their defensive posture, and even that one shot came on a power play.

A few seconds later, still with a man advantage, their second shot, by Geir Myhre, sailed beyond Jim Craig, the Americans' goalie.

But the Americans responded with three goals in the second period and two more in the final 20 min-utes.

"We had to become grinders, so to speak," said Brooks later. But he insisted there was "no screaming, no yelling" after the first period. "We had to get back our poise and our patience with the puck."

The Norwegian coach, Ronald Petterson, admitted when the game was over, "We tried to defend ourselves, because the lower the score the better chance we had to win."

But the Americans had ultimately too much talent and, at bottom, more reason to win. The Norwegians were virtually out of the running after their opening losses. The Americans stormed back in the seccond period, getting a goal after 41 seconds by Mike Eruzione. Craig immediately kept his team tied by halting Stephen Foyn's breakaway after Dave Christian lost his stick.

Soon, Mark Johnson converted Rob McClanahan's pass for a 2–1 edge and Dave Silk, a Ranger draft choice, made the score 3–1.

With only two seconds remaining in the period, Brooks did something rarely seen in the National Hockey League when a team is winning. He pulled his goalie. The reason? The faceoff was at the other end, making it virtually impossible for the Norsemen to score a goal if they gained the puck, but giving the Americans an extra skater inside the enemy territory.

The ploy failed, but it symbolized the innovative nature of the Americans' play.

In the final period, Mark Wells and his college teammate, Ken Morrow closed out the scoring.

Among those impressed with the Americans was Brian O'Neill, the N.H.L.'s executive vice president.

"The Americans skate as good as any team I've seen in a long time," he said.

A major reason play in the Games has been so dramatically quick was that the rink was 15 feet wider than the traditional ice surfaces. It is 100 feet wide and 200 feet long. This gives the skaters much more room to maneuver, to make plays, and to employ more of the ice for strategic alignments.

There remained, however, the old-fashioned key of emotion.

Before the game, Brooks warned his goalie, "The team will still be up in the clouds because of the Czech game, so watch out." As usual, Craig performed his watchdog duties well.

At game's end, tiny American flags sprouted, furiously shaken, as the crowd stood and applauded, and Brooks walked off behind his team, his emotions concealed behind narrowed eyes and pursed lips. Herb Brooks may have kept his hopes to himself, but many Americans were beginning to think about the still remote possibility of a gold medal.

★★★★ ★★★★★ ★★★★★ ★★★★★ ★★★★★

7: A YOUNG TEAM
THAT PLAYS LIKE VETS

★★★★★★★★★★ ★★★★ ★★★★★ ★★★★★

Gerald Eskenazi

They became known as Team U.S.A. They were players performing joyfully, with a collective identity under the influence of a driving coach.

They were, surprisingly, the still undefeated United States Olympic hockey team, tied for first place with Sweden in the Blue Division.

In an Olympics where empty seats are evident at many events, whenever the American hockey team played, scalpers stood outside and shouted. "Who needs hockey?" Meanwhile, fans on the prowl trudged through the snow, pleading, "Who's got hockey?" When scalper met buyer, a ticket costing $30—even to a lesser game, such as the last one against Norway— was sold for $50.

The fans knew that they would see the most exciting hockey of the day—a new American style that Coach Herb Brooks has orchestrated, with the traditional North American body checks blended with the European flow, with the United States players not afraid to be intuitive. The Americans kept the puck in play, and sometimes there was such a long time between whistles that the action was almost spellbinding.

The Americans exploited their own youthfulness. Brooks demanded that his players not worry about who had more experience—the other teams did, anyway—or who was stronger. He told them, "Use your youth."

That very youthfulness evoked standing ovations. Often, it appeared as if the fans had been watching one American line trying to outdo another. While there was also cheering at the other Olympic events, there was laughter in the stands at American hockey games.

People were happy as they sprouted flags and chanted, "U.S.A., U.S.A."

No matter what happened in a game Brooks did not permit his players to be at the postgame news conference. Brooks attended, typically sitting forward on a stage of the auditorium with shoulders hunched as if to spring at a nervy questioner.

Despite the team's success, the players cannot share the stage. The reasons were simple. Brooks refused to have any player singled out after a game, especially in an atmosphere where they might have been recipients of adulation from the news media in attendance. The coach wanted collective victories. And, perhaps as important, he did not want any player to believe that one team member was performing so well that there was no room for improvement.

After three games Brooks had not smiled, despite two victories and a tie. A key to the way he motivates his players is that he claims he is never satisfied, and that he must have more from his players. Somehow, they comply.

"Yes, it's applie pie," says an associate. "But Herb Brooks picked the sort of players that would listen to him, and go along with this."

Not all of them do it without reservation. Jim Craig, the goalie from Boston University, raises both eyebrows when asked about Brooks's techniques.

There are four Easterners on the club, all from the Boston school. From time to time, they complain about the "western" emphasis, how Brooks has selected eight people from his University of Minnesota team on a 20-man roster.

When asked about this Minnesota leaning, Brooks —who coached the team to the National Collegiate title last year—says, "I'm not going to cut my throat."

What he doesn't say is that he believes players from the West are better or that his college players are best of all. But while assembling the Olympic team in training camp last summer, the Easterners grumbled

31

whenever one of their number was cut. They were further distressed when, at a dinner for the American team, the band played the University of Minnesota fight song.

But to Mike Ramsey, an expert defender who played at Minnesota for Brooks, the players became united during a December tournament at the Olympic arena here.

"We went 4–0 and we won the tournament," Ramsey said. "O.K., it was against other countries' B teams, except for Canada. But after that there was the sense we could do it."

Yet, when Ramsey first looked at the schedule, he said, "Gee, if we get through this, we'll get through anything."

Brooks had set a schedule that some people thought would break his players. They started with 10 games in 16 days in the Netherlands, Finland and Switzerland. They finished their tour at Madison Square Garden, the 10–3 rout by the Russians. Some observers said that Brooks had gone too far, pitting impressionable youngsters against what may be the world's best hockey team only 72 hours before the Olympics opened.

That is not what Ramsey remembers. He tells you how, standing on the ice at the Garden, he heard the national anthem.

"They started cheering halfway through, and when they got to 'land of the free,' you couldn't even hear it any more. It sent chills down my spine. I have never experienced that before."

So he is not embarrassed to add, "With all the propaganda going on in the world, it feels good to represent the U.S.A."

In contrast to Ramsey, a Midwesterner, the four Easterners are seen as the more worldly members of the team.

Mike Eruzione perhaps typifies them. At the age of 25, he is one of the senior players, having been out of college since 1977. He spent two seasons with the

Toledo Blades of the International League, and his new teammates hang on his stories of life in a minor league. He keeps them relaxed in the locker room.

Craig, meanwhile, accepted the team's worries as the goalie. "I know I must have a good opening five minutes. I have to make the team feel at ease."

Although he yielded only six goals in the first three games, it was likely Brooks would rest him against Rumania and employ Steve Janaszak instead.

Players admitted that there was nothing in their experience to prepare them for the tension of the Olympics.

"It dawns on you," says another Bostonian, John O'Callahan. "You sit at your locker before the game. All of a sudden you realize where you are."

This shock of recognition may be the American theme.

One of the American Olympic committee members who helped select Brooks is Walter Bush, the vice president of the Minnesota North Stars.

"Brooks is helping them turn pro," Bush says. "He tells them, 'You've got to play hurt, you've got to take the bus trips.' "

★★★★★★★★★★★★★★★★★★★★★★★★★

8: THE RUMANIANS FALL

★★★★★★★★★★★★★★★★★★★★★★★★★

Gerald Eskenazi

It was not merely a victory. It was not simply the fact that the final score was a definitive 7–2. Nor was it the momentum that the team gained by winning its third game in a row.

With its most effective performance of the XIII Olympic Winter Games, the surprising United States hockey team truly took charge. And it moved closer to the medal round by routing Rumania.

The undefeated Americans, who then had three victories and a tie, had one opening-round game remaining, a contest against the West German team.

With a victory over West Germany, the Americans would be assured of being one of the top two teams in the Blue Division and thus of advancing to the final round to compete for medals. The Americans would also advance if Sweden beat or tied Czechoslovakia.

Buzz Schneider and Eric Strobel scored for the United States in the first period against Rumania. The Americans led by 4–1 after two periods, with Mark Wells and Schneider having scored, while Steve Christoff, Neal Broten and Rob McClanahan got goals in the third period.

Still, Craig Patrick, the assistant coach of the United States team, was not satisfied with a performance that left most of the 8,500 fans either hoarse from cheering or weary from waving flagpole-sized flags.

Patrick, who worked behind the bench with Coach Herb Brooks, contended that the Americans had not played with the same enthusiasm they had displayed in two of their opening games, the unexpected tie with Sweden and the upset victory over Czechoslovakia.

Craig was perhaps reflecting the attitude of his hard-to-please boss, for this was the most intelligent game the young United States team had played. The Americans worked play after play to perfection, taking good, close shots. It was the sort of passing and puck control that Brooks had been trying to teach his players.

The United States team also got another outstanding display of goaltending by Jim Craig, whom Brooks had wanted to rest. But Craig had other plans and, according to Patrick, "We've got to keep him happy."

Craig was superb in the Winter Games, following a distressing two weeks leading to the Olympics that turned the normally placid netminder into a worrier. But as soon as the first Olympic puck was dropped, he became the squad's most effective player.

As a result, the Americans were able to concentrate on attacking. That was an advantage because one of the determining factors in which teams advance, or how ties are broken, could be the difference in goals scored and goals against. The Swedes were plus 17 to the Americans' plus 13.

Those complicating factors were hardly on the minds of the fans as they revelled in the nonstop play that had become the American team's symbol.

The Rumanians, who wore their canary yellow tops and royal blue pants and looked somewhat like a softball team, concentrated on playing defensive hockey. They did not go out of their way to take a shot as long as they could prevent an American drive.

There was little the Rumanians could do, however. Only the Americans' failure to convert on several remarkable chances kept the score from running into double digits. The Americans smacked 51 shots at Valerian Netedu, while Craig saw only 21. In this case, the shots correctly told the story of the game.

But there was another sort of story: the Cone Line. That was the castoff trio of Buzz Schneider, the 25-year-old perpetual amateur who was supposed to be over the hill, John Harrington, and Mark Pavelich. The line's nickname referred to the paper cones that schoolteachers used to put on the heads of students who did badly—the trio's teammates thought they would be an ineffective line. Instead Schneider led the team with four goals.

Schneider opened the scoring midway through the opening session against the Rumanians on a tic-tac-toe play that started when Pavelich stole the puck and brought it up with Harrington. The play ended with Schneider's slashing drive.

By then, the fans had finished shoving one another in a late dash for their seats. At game time, hundreds of the plastic red seats were empty as fans had been stalled on the stairwells.

To get to their seats, fans had to give their tickets to ushers, who stood on the top of the stairs. As a guard took a ticket, ripped off the stub and handed it back, delays were created. The situation worsened because some people also had press passes, with which the ushers were not familiar. While the ushers scrutinized the passes, people below were in danger of being shoved down the stairs. Lines were solid from the outside of the building through the doorway and up the stairway.

That was only one aspect of the poor planning in what was the fourth day that hockey games were staged in the Olympic Field House. There were patches of dark blue on the ice, which was tinted to aid television. On opening night, the chemicals somehow turned the blue lines red; during the Rumanian game they were a purplish-brown.

Meanwhile, up above, the press box was dark. The only ceiling lights were over the ice. Fans not only had trouble reading their programs, which cost $5, but they also had trouble hearing what the public-address announcer said. The fans, of course, were cheering so wildly during the game with Rumania that it probably did not matter.

The lighting apparently did not bother Craig, who

in the last two games yielded only one goal with both teams at even strength. That goal came after Wells had increased the Americans' edge to 3–0. Doru Tureanu of Rumania, on a power play, then cut the score to 3–1. But Schneider, with a whistling slap shot, gave the Americans a 4–1 margin.

During the third period, Steve Christoff, assisted by Jack O'Callahan, Neal Broten, assisted by Mike Eruzione, and Rob McClanahan, assisted by Mark Johnson, scored goals to bring the final tally to 7–2.

★★★★★★★★★★★★★★★★★★★★★★★★

9: ICE HOCKEY THE RUSSIAN WAY: THE BACKGROUND

★★★★★★★★★★ ★★★★★★★★★★★★★

Dave Anderson

In the noontime chill of the old Olympic Arena, the noise sounded like gunfire. Hockey pucks cracked against the Plexiglas, boomed against the wooden boards and stuttered against the goaltender's leather pads.

This was the Soviet Union team in rehearsal. The joke among hockey people is that the Russians' practices are better than most teams' games, even National Hockey League games. But it was not a joke to those teams that had to play them in the Olympic tournament.

"They are," said one N.H.L. visitor, "like a skunk at a garden party."

As they awaited their game with Finland, the Russians were the Olympics' only unbeaten, untied and unmerciful team. They had strafed Japan, 16–0, and the Netherlands, 17–4, before their 8–1 triumph over Poland, when half a dozen anti-Soviet political banners were confiscated. Unless the ice melted, or unless the United States team or another team performed a miracle, as did the American squad in 1960, the Russians were expected to win the Olympic gold medal for the sixth time in the last seven tournaments.

"But this is a very unusual practice for them," a long-time observer of the Russians was saying now. "Not everybody is working out."

On the ice for practice, only 13 players had joined Viktor Tikhonov, the coach, and Vladimir Jurzinov, his assistant, who resembled Santa Claus elves in their floppy stocking caps. But the other seven players, including the 35-year-old captain and center, Boris Mikhailov, were in the stands. Throughout its Olympic stay, the Soviet team was quietly guarded by New

York State troopers alert for anti-Soviet political demonstrators.

Bundled in thick red jackets and pants, the other seven players were not sprawled in repose. Instead, they were leaning forward on the edges of their red plastic chairs, watching their teammates perspire as intently as the several dozen aficionados who had wandered in to view technique the way medical students study surgeons at work.

Inside the blue line, 30-year-old Valery Vasilev, the Russians' best defenseman, was hunched over like a puma in a tree. From the side boards, the young defenseman, Viacheslav Fetisov, slid him passes as Viktor Tikhonov watched.

One after another, at intervals of three to four seconds at the most, Valery Vasilev slammed slap shots at 27-year-old Vladislav Tretyak, the Russians' celebrated goaltender, who blocked most of them. But of the 10 shots, only one was wide of the net. And when Valery Vasilev shot, he never hesitated, he never missed connecting solidly with the puck. When he shot, it was all one motion, the same way that, in the Russian translation, "icehockey" is all one word.

That "icehockey" history goes back only about 35 years. Not until after World War II did the Russians hold their first national championships. Not until 1956 did they enter a team in the Olympics, the year they won their first gold medal.

The official version of that history is contained in the 56-page "icehockey" section of a 211-page "The USSR Olympic Team" media guide, in both Russian and English, with a hard red cover that is available here in the headquarters of Tass, the official Soviet press agency. Its propaganda is obvious.

But the guide also supports the theory of some N.H.L.-oriented hockey people that a Communist system lends itself to a team game better than a star system does.

"Soviet icehockey," it says in the Olympic Guide, "has been developing since its first years in a peculiar way. Those who inaugurated the game in the country played other games and above all football and bandy. They helped to form the school of Soviet icehockey which prompted icehockey as a game of collective and combinational tactics in a high tempo."

In addition to their five Olympic gold medals, the Russians had competed in 24 world and European championships, winning 16 world titles and 19 European titles. In those tournaments, the Russians had won 176 games, tied 10 and lost only 23 while scoring 1,492 goals to the opposition's 394 goals. The guide acknowledges that Canada has won more world championships, but adds, "the players of the country where the game of icehockey originated participated in 35 world championships."

The development of the Russians is best understood in the overwhelming number of its players, facilities and instructors. According to its Olympic guide, the Soviet Union has:

- 260,077 physical education collectives in the enterprises, construction sites, institutions, collective farms and Soviet farms, and schools that have ice hockey sections.
- 749,940 players who go in for ice hockey in those sections.
- 287,291 ice hockey players who have offcial sports categories; 6,461 of them are athletes of the 1st grade or Candidates for Masters of Sport.
- 211 ice hockey players who are Masters of Sport or Masters of Sport, International Class.
- 986 full-time coaches who train the qualified ice hockey players.
- 50,469 unpaid public instructors who train the ice hockey players of mass grading.
- 14,460 ice hockey rinks that are at disposal of those who are practicing the game.
- 55,637 referees who umpire ice hockey matches.

Those numbers, of course, are consistent with the Soviet philosophy that "physical education and sports become one of the most popular forms of active rest

40

among the people" in a nation with a population of 265 million. But sometimes a hockey player is a hockey player is a hockey player. During practice, as Valery Vasilev stood motionless near center ice for a moment, he yawned. The coach was looking the other way.

10: THE AMERICANS ADVANCE . . .
Gerald Eskenazi

The United States, with the youngest hockey squad in the XIII Olympic Winter Games, advanced to the medal round of four teams. To the cynics, it was a pyrrhic victory. The real test against the Russians was yet to be met.

The Americans got an assist in making it to the medal round from Sweden, which upset Czechoslovakia 4–2. That result guaranteed an American finish of no lower than second place in the Blue Division.

Although the United States beat West Germany, 4–2, to wind up undefeated and tied with Sweden at four victories and a tie, the Swedes finished first in the division because of a better goals-differential record, the element for breaking ties in the standing. It meant the United States would play the undefeated and untied Soviet Union squad, the Red Division winner. Four teams—the first two finishers in each of the two divisions—were to begin play Friday night for the gold, silver and bronze medals. The other team from the Red Division would be Finland, which beat the Netherlands, 10–3. Although Canada and Finland finished with 3-2 records, the Finns advanced on the basis of having beaten Canada in their meeting.

Perhaps because they sensed they had little chance at finishing in first place, the Americans were at their most physical in the game with West Germany, especially after trailing in the first period.

They went into the game needing not only a victory to tie the Swedes for first place, but needing to win by more than six goals to have a better goals-differential than the Swedes. The Swedes had plus-19, meaning they had scored 19 more goals than they had allowed. The United States took the ice with a plus-13

★★★★★★★★★★★★★★★★★
THEY SKATED FOR THE GOLD AND GLORY
★★★★★★★★★★★★★★★★★
"Over two weeks in February
a bunch of American kids went after
the best hockey teams in the
world, and beat the pants off them."
—THE NEW YORK TIMES

On February 9, 1980,
two weeks before the Olympic
confrontation, the grim
American players watched their
team lose to the Russians.
(NEW YORK TIMES)

**Team America's first Olympic game with Sweden.
Mike Eruzione watches the puck slide past Sweden's
goalie for the game-tying score.**
(BARTON SILVERMAN/NEW YORK TIMES)

Ken Morrow (left) and Buzz Schneider of the United States are thwarted in a first period scoring attempt against Sweden.
(BARTON SILVERMAN/NEW YORK TIMES)

Bill Baker brings the crowd
to its feet by
scoring America's first
goal in the game
against Sweden,
tying the score, 1-1.
(BARTON SILVERMAN /
NEW YORK TIMES)

Buzz Schneider scores a goal during
the game against Czechoslovakia.
The final score showed the U.S. on top, 7–3. (UPI)

Mark Wells scores in the third period against Norwegian goalie, Jim Martinsen.
(BARTON SILVERMAN/NEW YORK TIMES)

A battle almost erupted when David Silk
and Geir Myhre of Norway
nearly came to blows at the Norwegian cage.
(EDWARD HAUSNER/NEW YORK TIMES)

Buzz Schneider's scoring attempt
is thwarted by the goalie in the first period of
the game against Romania.
Later, Schneider scored twice.
(BARTON SILVERMAN / NEW YORK TIMES)

Buzz Schneider of the U.S. slams
one of his two goals past Romania's Gheorshe Hutan.
The U.S. defeated Romania by a score of 7–2. (UPI)

United States goalie Jim Craig
is surrounded by familiar faces—teammates
Bill Baker (left) and Dave Christian.
(DAVID MOIR)

Dave Silk watches Rob McClanahan's
shot elude goalie Sigmund Süttner for the
United States' third goal in
the third period against West Germany.
(BARTON SILVERMAN/NEW YORK TIMES)

Ken Morrow, a 23-year-old defenseman from Davison, Michigan, scored two goals and had one assist in the Olympics.
(DAVID MOIR)

U.S.A. vs. U.S.S.R.—second period
Mark Johnson is ecstatic after scoring
the team's second goal.
(BARTON SILVERMAN / NEW YORK TIMES)

Jim Craig: "The pressure was unbearable.
But we had a good thing goin' for us." Craig makes
one of his 36 saves on 39 Soviet shots
on goal during the game.
(EDWARD HAUSNER/NEW YORK TIMES)

Phil Verchota scored the tying
goal in the third period of the final game
against Finland.
(DAVID MOIR)

Mark Pavelich, a hard-skating center
from Eveleth, Minnesota, had two assists in
the triumph over the Soviet Union. (DAVID MOIR)

As tempers flared,
Mike Eruzione
was restrained by officials
when U.S. and
Soviet players almost
came to blows.
(EDWARD HAUSNER/NEW YORK TIMES

**Dave Christian, whose family
has now collected three Olympic gold medals,
led the United States in assists.**
(DAVID MOIR)

An all-American at Boston University,
Jack O'Callahan was one of
the team's most reliable defensemen.
(DAVID MOIR)

In the second period of the game
with the Soviet Union, Jim Craig makes
one of his spectacular saves.
(EDWARD HAUSNER/NEW YORK TIMES)

Eric Strobel scored a crucial goal
against Romania and collected an assist each
against West Germany and Norway.
(DAVID MOIR)

Buzz Schneider, at 25
the oldest member of the team, had
four goals and three assists,
tying him with Mark Johnson as the
leading scorer. (DAVID MOIR)

Soviet goalie Vladimir Myshkin sees the puck
fly past him as Mike Eruzione scores the winning
point during the third period.
(BARTON SILVERMAN / NEW YORK TIMES)

The final countdown. Soviet (left) and
American (right) teams and coaches watch the clock
in the final seconds of the game. U.S. wins 4–3! (AP)

Players on the bench exult after 4–3 victory over the Soviet Union. (BARTON SILVERMAN/NEW YORK TIMES)

"It's like a bunch of Canadian college football players beating the Pittsburgh Steelers."
—Jim Craig. (BARTON SILVERMAN / NEW YORK TIMES)

"We're all a bunch of big doolies, now!"
—**Mike Eruzione** (BARTON SILVERMAN / NEW YORK TIMES)

And on the other side...
defeat on the faces
of officials of
the Soviet Union's
Olympic hockey team. (UPI)

Coach Herb Brooks receives a call from President Carter after the U.S. victory over the Soviet Union. "These people are deserving because of their age and what they had to accomplish in a short time."—Coach Brooks (AP)

Goalie Jim Craig, after Finland scored
its second goal and moved ahead
of the U.S., 2–1. "My men were diving,
blocking them with their bodies,
blocking them with their heads, anything."
—Jim Craig (EDWARD HAUSNER/NEW YORK TIMES)

Goalie Valtonen stands defeated after Mark Johnson scored the clinching goal in the 4–2 victory over Finland. (UPI)

"We deserved it. We deserved every bleepin', bleepin'
bit ot it."—Jim Craig (BARTON SILVERMAN/NEW YORK TIMES)

"We knew we were younger, we knew we could
outskate them, we knew we were going to break
our butts to beat 'em."—Mark Johnson
(EDWARD HAUSNER/NEW YORK TIMES)

Jubilant U.S. hockey players celebrate with fans on the ice as the clock ran out and they beat Finland for the gold medal. (BARTON SILVERMAN/NEW YORK TIMES)

"The saddest thing for me right now
is that after the President's
dinner… we just go our different ways."—Mike Eruzione
(BARTON SILVERMAN/NEW YORK TIMES)

Neal Broten raises his arms in triumph after
receiving his gold medal.
(BARTON SILVERMAN/NEW YORK TIMES)

"No way we weren't gonna wrap up the gold."
—Mike Ramsey (BARTON SILVERMAN/NEW YORK TIMES)

"We all came together six months ago from different ethnic beliefs...and we made ourselves a team."
—Mike Eruzione (BARTON SILVERMAN/NEW YORK TIMES)

The golden victory: U.S.A. 4—Finland 2.
"They have startled the athletic world.
Not just the hockey world.
The athletic world."—Coach Brooks (UPI)

"I can't believe they called me from
the White House and asked me what I wanted to eat.
I told them I wanted two lobsters...
after all, we did beat the Red Tide."—Jim Craig (UPI)

On February 12, twenty Americans
stepped onto the Olympic ice—their
team seeded 7th among the
12 national squads. On February 24,
they stepped off as number one,
draped in Old Glory. (AP)

mark and finished the five-game preliminary series with a plus-15.

The West Germans looked sharper not only in their red-and-black uniforms, but also in their first-period play as they took a 2–0 lead. On a 65-foot slap shot by Horst-Peter Kretschmer, Jim Craig was moving the wrong way in the American goal. On a 50-foot slap shot by Udd Aiessling off a power-play faceoff, Craig did not move at all.

A breakaway goal by Bob McClanahan, and Neil Broten's drive from the slot tied the score in the second period, evoking the suddenly traditional chants of "U.S.A." and flag-waving. McClanahan's second goal of the game, in the final period, lifted the Americans to a 3–2 lead. Then Phil Verchota deflected home Dave Christian's slap shot for the 4–2 advantage.

But that still left the United States five goals shy of taking first place, and the lineup for the start of medal play looked like this: The United States against the Soviet Union in the 5 P.M. opener, followed by the Sweden-Finland game.

Then, two days later, the Americans were to meet Finland at 11 A.M. and the Russians were to battle the Swedes at 2:30 P.M.

The Americans would take 1 point into the final round, for the tie they earned against the Swedes. Sweden likewise had a point in the medal round. The Soviet team had 2 points, since they beat Finland in their round robin, and the Finns had none.

Thus, the United States could guarantee itself a bronze medal, at least, by defeating Finland on Sunday, since that would give the Americans at least 3 points, while the most the Finns could earn would be 2. The West German coach, Hans Rampf, was not very sanguine about the Americans' chances against the Russians—if they played as they did against the Germans. "The question is who the referee is," he explained. The coach contended there were many penalties not called against the United States.

"If they get penalties against the Russians they won't have a chance," Rampf said. "They'll have to stay on the ice and not the penalty box."

. . . In a Splendid Competition
Red Smith

Despite hideously tangled traffic and frustrated customers and empty seats, the Olympic competition was splendid. And not the least attractive was the performance of the United States' almost beardless hockey team. (Ken Morrow, the defenseman drafted by the New York Islanders, has whiskers that starlings could nest in, but some of his playmates have yet to feel a razor on their damask pelts.)

With two games still to play against the menacing Soviet six and the skillful Finns, Team Adolescence was undefeated with four victories and a tie. The young Yanks still faced with the Russians who walloped them, 10–3, in Madison Square Garden in a pre-Olympics tune-up, the Russians who were unbeaten and considered unbeatable here.

Then the Americans play Finland. Regardless of the Soviet-American result, a victory over the Finns would guarantee a bronze medal—only the second blob of hardware for the Americans since upstarts coached by Jack Riley of the United States Military Academy swept the 1960 tournament.

In 1972, Americans took a silver medal behind the Russians, but in other Games since 1960 they finished fifth, sixth and fourth while the Soviet Union cleaned everybody's clock.

"And don't forget," said Herb Brooks, the American coach, "eight of their players here were on the Soviet team that played Team Canada [of the National Hockey League] in 1972. At that time, about 12 of our kids were playing peewee hockey."

Before the trouble started, the United States was seeded no better than seventh and Brooks said, "A bronze medal here would be the equivalent of a gold in 1960."

"I know my players are tired of hearing me say it," he said on another occasion, "but I have to keep telling them we don't have the talent to win games here. We have to do it on talent, work, cohesion and rhythm." He did not add "and coaching."

It was taken more or less for granted that Brooks's brawny babes would bomb out early, for they were matched at the start with Sweden, seeded third, and Czechoslovakia, ranked second. Bill Baker, captain of Brooks's 1979 team at the University of Minnesota, scored the tying goal against Sweden with 27 seconds to play. Hardly knowing their own strength, the jubilant kids then creamed the Czechoslovaks, 7–3.

In spite of victories over Norway and Rumania, Brooks still saw ghosties and ghoulies in his sleep, still heard things that go bump in the night. "I'm scared to death of West Germany," he said. "I always have been, because they always give us trouble in key games." He was thinking of 1976 in Innsbruck, when West Germany's 4–1 score on the last day cost the United States a bronze.

So they faced off against the West Germans while flags waved in the stands, bedsheet banners exhorted the Yanks, fans bawled and chanted and beat their palms. Less than two minutes later, America was trailing, 1–0, and Brooks was breathing hard.

Forty-five seconds before the first period ended, Udo Kiessling was screened out of Craig's view. The goalie never saw the puck until it was in the net and the score was 2–0.

"I hate it when I can't see the puck," said Craig, who once was a catcher in baseball. "I like to lock in on it and follow it. I hate not being ready. When a shot is screened, it really terrifies me."

More aggressive and more physical than the West Germans, Craig's comrades bombarded Sig Suttner's net, but that goalie could stop the common cold. "Let's go, U.S.A.!" the galleries chanted. Bob McClanahan

45

responded with a goal. Neil Broten scored. The second period ended with a tie. McClanahan drove another home in the third period. A shot by David Christian caromed off Phil Verchota's stick, and that was it, 4–2.

"I am sure," said the West German coach, Hans Rampf, "that the United States will go into the next two matches with great spirit, but they still have to work very concentrated. Much depends on the officials, because I thought the Americans should have had five more penalties than they had against us.

"I would never say they played dirty. They worked hard, and when a man does that, fouls happen. It is the referee's duty to call them. If he does, the Americans will never get a chance against Russia."

"We can't make a mistake all night," said Craig Patrick, the American assistant coach. "This is for all the money—well, not money, all the glory."

Between the conquest of West Germany and the confrontation with the Russians, one contest was fought to a decision. The American Broadcasting Company wanted the key match rescheduled from 5 P.M. to 8:30 P.M. so it could be televised live.

Television can move a championship fight from New York to Las Vegas. It can switch World Series games to prime time and put Bowie Kuhn into thermal underwear. Television cannot control the International Ice Hockey Federation.

The show must go on, at 5.

★★★★★★★★ ★★★★★★★★★★★★★

11: UNITED STATES 4 —
SOVIET UNION 3

★★★★★★★★ ★★★★★★★★★★★★★

Gerald Eskenazi

In one of the most startling and dramatic upsets
in Olympic history, the underdog United States hockey
team, composed in great part of collegians, defeated
the defending champion Soviet squad by 4–3.

The victory brought a congratulatory phone call
to the dressing room from President Carter and set off
fireworks over the tiny Adirondack village. The triumph also put the Americans in a commanding position to take the gold medal in the XIII Olympic Winter
Games.

If the United States defeated Finland, which tied
Sweden, 3–3, the Americans would win the gold medal
regardless of the outcome of the game between Sweden
and the Soviet Union later that day. If the United
States tied Finland, the Americans were assured of at
least a bronze medal.

The American goal that broke a 3–3 tie against
the Russians was scored midway through the final
period by a player who typified the makeup of the
United States team.

His name is Mike Eruzione, he is from Winthrop,
Mass., he is the American team's captain and he was
plucked from obscurity. His opponents included world-
renowned stars, some of them performing in the Olympics for the third time.

The Soviet team had captured five of the last six
Olympics. The only club to defeat them since 1956
was the United States team of 1960, which won the
gold medal at Squaw Valley, Calif.

Few victories in American Olympic play have
provoked reaction comparable to that provoked by the
decision in the red-seated, smallish Olympic Field
House at the end of the United States-Soviet Union

game. At the final buzzer, after the fans had chanted the seconds away, fathers and mothers and friends of the United States players dashed onto the ice, hugging everyone they could find in red, white and blue uniforms. Truly, they had witnessed a miracle on ice.

Meanwhile, in the stands, most of the 10,000 fans—including about 1,500 standees, who paid $24.40 apiece for a ticket—shouted "U.S.A." over and over, and hundreds outside waved American flags. Later, the orchestrator of the team, Coach Herb Brooks took out a yellow piece of paper, displayed the almost illegible scrawl on it, and said, "I really said this to the guys. I'm not lying to you."

Before the game, Brooks had taken out that card in the locker room and read his remarks.

"You were born to be a player," he read. "You were meant to be here." They proved him right.

From the opening minutes fans and players fed off one another in the festive atmosphere at the arena. The tempo and emotion of the game was established early, when a longtime Soviet star, Valery Kharlamov, wearing the traditional lipstick-red uniform, was sandwiched between two Americans.

Suddenly, he was lifted between them and, looking like a squirt of ketchup, sailed into the air and then flopped to the ice. Beyond the constant pressure of intimidating body checks, though, were the intricate passing patterns of the Americans, who have derived many of their techniques from the Russians.

The Soviet system is based on attack. The Russians more than doubled the shots on goal of the Americans, 39–16, but almost every one that the Russians took was stopped, often dramatically, by Jim Craig.

As a result of the victory, the hockey players would be among the prouder contingents of the 150 American Olympians to be honored at the White House at a two-hour session with the President.

The Americans struggled until the final period, however, never leading until Eruzione's goal. They trailed by 3–2 going into the last 20-minute period. No hockey game is played nonstop for 60 minutes, but this one came close. The Russians have been famed for their conditioning techniques. They also were considered the finest hockey team in the world.

The Soviet Union broke through first, with its new young star, Valery Krutov, getting his stick in the way of Aleksei Kasatonov's whistling slap shot. The puck changed direction and sailed beyond Craig's reach in the first period.

Midway through the period, the only American who has been an Olympian, Buzz Schneider, drilled a shot over the left shoulder of Vladislav Tretyak, the Soviet goalie.

The goal was Schneider's fifth of the series, giving him the team lead. That is a surprising performance for a player who once failed the tryout with the lowly Pittsburgh Penguins in the National League, and since has bounced around American leagues of less stature.

But there were other highlights of that first period. The Russians had one when Sergei Makarov punched the puck past Craig while fans screamed in vain for Referee Karl-Gustav Kaisla of Finland to notice an American who was being held.

Only a few seconds remained when Ken Morrow slammed an 80-foot desperation shot toward the goal. The puck caromed out to Mark Johnson, who struck it home with no seconds showing on the clock.

A goal cannot be scored with no time remaining. Actually, when the puck had sailed in there was a second left. It took another second for the goal judge to press the button signaling the score and stopping the clock.

The Soviet skaters left the ice, contending time was over, but after Kaisla spoke to other officials, the goal was allowed. The arena rocked with applause with the verification of the 2–2 tie.

Back came the disappointed Russians from their dressing room, adjusting their shiny red helmets. They had a new player on the ice, too—Vladimir Myshkin had replaced Tretyak in goal for the final faceoff of the period. Later, the assistant Soviet coach, Vladimir Jursinov, explained the removal of Tretyak, saying through an interpreter, "He is not playing well and my feeling is he is nervous."

Myshkin kept the Americans at bay for the second period, although they tested him with only two shots. The Russians took a 3–2 lead when one of their veterans, Aleksandr Maltsev, scored with a man advantage.

But in the last period Johnson swatted home a shot that Dave Silk had gotten off while being hauled down, and the puck eluded Myshkin to tie the score. About a minute and a half later, with exactly half of the period over, Eruzione picked up a loose puck in the Soviet zone, skated to a point between the faceoff circles and fired a screened, 30-foot shot through the pads of Myshkin for the winning score.

The goal set off cheering that lasted through the remainder of the game, as the youngest team of all the American squads, average age 22, put itself in a position to win only the second gold medal ever for an American hockey team.

. . . And the Fireworks Explode
Dave Anderson

Outside the Olympic Field House, fireworks exploded above Main Street in the tiny Adirondack Mountain village of Lake Placid. Four searchlights lit up the dark sky. On the snow-muddied sidewalks, thousands of people stood around, still transfixed by the United States's 4–3 upset of the Soviet Union in the XIII Winter Olympics hockey tournament. To most hockey people, the Soviet national team was the world's best team, better than any National Hockey League team.

But the best team lost.

A platoon of Americans, mostly from colleges in cold-weather states like Minnesota and Massachusetts, ambushed the renowned Soviet national team gathered from the Central Red Army and the Moscow Wings and the Moscow Dynamo, virtually the same Soviet players who had embarrassed the N.H.L. all-stars in the Challenge Cup at Madison Square Garden a year ago.

Throughout the second game against the Russians, the chant of "U.S.A., U.S.A." appeared to inspire the American team as it had throughout the Olympic tournament. And all through the small arena that has only 8,500 seats, dozens of American flags, large and small, had been waved.

When the game finally ended, the spectators who had paid up to $67.40 for a seat at center ice—if not $150 to a scalper—stood and shouted as American players jumped and hugged each other while the Soviets grouped silently at the other end of the ice, staring in shock at the scene around them.

Now, outside the arena, the "U.S.A., U.S.A." chant could be heard every so often—from down Main Street past the speed-skating oval, from the lot where the buslines were, from a third-floor window in Lake Placid High School that serves as the Olympic press center.

Near the players' entrance, goalie Jim Craig was surrounded by people who unknowingly were shoving him toward one of the arena's huge plate-glass windows. In the game he had stopped 36 shots, including nine in the third period as the Americans rallied for two goals. But now he appeared to be unnerved by the plate-glass window and the fireworks bursting above.

"Hey, don't push me into the window," he was saying now. "Don't push me into the window."

But then he talked about the Soviets' desperate rushes for the tying goal they never obtained.

"They panicked at the end," he said. "I couldn't

51

believe it. They were just throwing the puck in and hoping for a break. Hey, what was the final score? Was it 4–3? Does anybody know the final score?"

Yes, it was 4–3, he was told.

"That was my kind of game," he said. "I had to concentrate all the way. My ear was hurting from the flu I've had the last few days. I took a penicillin shot but I wouldn't let myself believe I could get sick. I'll get sick next week."

Just as he was asked a question, a dazzle of fireworks burst high in the sky, startling him.

"Would you please repeat that question?" he said.

"Would you please repeat that question?"

Against the Soviets, he had resembled a goaltender carved in ice. But now he appeared frightened by the fireworks bursting above him.

"Would you please repeat that question?" he said again.

"How did you feel in there at the end?" he was asked.

"If we lost," he finally replied, "I was determined they would have to beat me with a good goal—all I was trying to do was keep us in the game. We were just lucky we got the breaks."

Not far away Mark Johnson, who scored the Americans' second and third goals, was wearing his red-white-and-blue jacket.

"I can't believe it. I can't believe we beat them. But we did. And now we're only 60 minutes away from the gold medal, baby, only 60 minutes away."

The United States still had to face Finland, a game that was to be followed by the Soviet Union-Sweden showdown in the afternoon.

"We only had two shots on net in the second period," Mark Johnson continued. "But we were only losing by 3–2 and that's when we knew we had a chance to win. When we lost to the Russians, 10–3, two weeks ago at Madison Square Garden, we were down 7–1 after two periods. But being behind by only one goal this time we knew we were younger, we knew

52

we could outskate them, we knew we were going to break our butts to beat 'em. And we did." Mike Eruzione, the American captain, scored the winning goal.

"On a line change too," the 25-year-old left-winger said from under the brim of his Olympic cowboy hat. "My buddy Buzz Schneider came off early, so I was out there with John Harrington and Mark Pavelich when Harrington gave me the puck inside the blue line. I shot, the defenseman screened the goaltender, and it went in. Very simple."

"Did the Afghanistan situation affect you?" somebody asked.

"That doesn't concern us now," he said. "All we're concerned about now is winning this tournament. Hey, we had champagne in our locker room but nobody touched it. We put it away until after Sunday's game. This is a dream that nobody can say they're a part of except us." And except all those people chanting, "U.S.A., U.S.A."

12: RECOGNITION AND RESPECT

Gerald Eskenazi

Suddenly, the United States hockey players had names. And their identities, which had been carefully concealed by their coach, surfaced.

In the early hours of the morning after the game, this morning, people at Mr. Mike's Pizza on Main Street, beer glasses raised, spoke of Mike Eruzione and Mark Johnson and Buzz Schneider and Jim Craig.

They and their teammates were only 60 minutes from a gold medal at the Olympic Games, which would be one of the more memorable achievements in Olympic history.

A victory over Finland, in a game that would be televised live, would guarantee the United States the gold medal no matter what happened in the second game between Sweden and the Soviet Union.

Symbolically, or perhaps simply bowing to the pressure exerted by newsmen, Coach Herb Brooks permitted his players to attend a news conference the day after their victory over the Soviet team—the first time he had done so. Sinister motives for keeping them hidden had been laid to Brooks. Some even believed it was because he wanted to keep the limelight to himself. However, there was nothing unusual about such a policy for Brooks. As a rule, he had appeared only after losses and had never made his players available at conferences.

Brooks was thought to have been a possible next coach of the New York Rangers, who have a tangled situation. Coach Fred Shero was thought to want to step down after this season, his second, to concentrate on his duties as general manager. His designated replacement, Mike Nykoluk, was joined by another assistant coach, André Beaulieu. If Brooks did not fit into the clouded picture and was not guaranteed a top spot with the Rangers, he might return to coaching at the University of Minnesota.

The Brooks situation was as difficult to discern as the Olympic playoff system, which was as follows: The Americans, who brought 1 point to the medal round from a tie with Sweden in the previous five-game round-robin, added 2 points by defeating the Soviet Union. A triumph over Finland would give them 5 and the gold medal because none of the other three teams could amass 5 points.

However, it was also possible for the Americans to have finished fourth and be shut out of any medals. Sweden, with 2 points—including 1 for a 3–3 tie with Finland—was to play the Soviet Union. The Russians also had 2 points, which they gained in the round-robin by beating Finland. The Finns had 1 point.

Anything could have happened then, including a four-way tie in points if the United States lost and Sweden and the Russians tied. If the four teams were tied with 3 points apiece, the winner would be the one with the greater differential between goals scored and goals allowed. If two teams, such as the United States and Sweden, tied for a medal, the winner would be the one that won the head-to-head meeting. If there were still a tie, the team that permitted fewer goals would win.

That was one reason Craig, the goaltender, had become the Americans' most important player. He was expected to be joining the Atlanta Flames in the near future, perhaps as a backup goalie, perhaps to be assigned to a minor league team.

For the time being, though, he was following his pre-Olympics schedule of permitting "three goals or fewer in every game." The Americans were undefeated overall with five victories and a tie. Only twice had teams touched Craig for three goals.

"I love playing in front of a crowd for or against me," said Craig. But "for" is better, he added. Of the 12 teams that began the tournament, there is only one home team—Craig's.

If the game against the Soviet Union had been contested at Sapporo, Japan, or Innsbruck, Austria, sites of previous Winter Olympics, would American emotions have been as high? Would fans have chanted and shouted as they did? Would fireworks have exploded over the mountaintops? Would hundreds of fans have waited for a glimpse of their heroes.

The emotional factor cannot be overlooked. Generally, Winter Games are not played in countries that have contending hockey teams, so every team is on neutral ice.

That was the story of Schneider's hockey life; every place he had been since getting out of the University of Minnesota had been neutral ice.

"I tried to play pro," said Schneider, craggy-featured and 25, the oldest player on the team. "I was the only player in the Pittsburgh Penguins' camp without a contract. They only needed me as a body to work out with. Then they cut me. Let's see, I've been to Hershey, then Saginaw, then Oklahoma City, Birmingham Bulls, Hampton, Springfield, and Europe."

Schneider led the American scorers with five goals. But last year he was ready to quit the game.

"I needed money," he explained. Although he was paid, he didn't sign a pro contract and thus retained his amateur standing. "Anyway, I would have paid them to play," he said. "If I can't get an N.H.L. contract after this is done, my wife and I are going to have to sit down and discuss our future. It's hard on her, all this moving."

Schneider, the only former Olympian on the squad, was overshadowed before the Games by Mark Johnson, considered the team's best player. Johnson is an intelligent, smallish center from the University of Wisconsin. He was coached by his father, who also coached the 1976 United States team, and was overlooked by most N.H.L. teams in the 1977 draft. They were worried about his size, 5 feet 9 inches and 160 pounds. Finally, the Penguins took him on the third round.

In 1978–79 Johnson was named the National Collegiate player of the year. He still has a year of college eligibility remaining.

At the news conference, the entire team was on the stage of the auditorium at Lake Placid High School. Coach Brooks would not say publicly why he had barred his players from public acclaim, but privately he admitted that it was because he wanted them thinking of themselves as a team, greater than any individual.

Eruzione, who had been chosen from the Toledo Gold Diggers of the International League, was surprised when asked whether the Americans had been lucky against the Russians, or whether the Russians had simply played poorly.

"I thought we were pretty good," he said.

Now the victory apparently had Brooks worried that his players may think it was for the championship.

Craig understood that, too.

"If we don't win tomorrow, people will forget," he said.

★★★★★★★★★★★★★★★★★★★★★★★★★

13: GLORIOUS GOLD

★★★★★★★★★★★★★★★★★★★★★★★★★

Gerald Eskenazi

The come-from-behind United States hockey team completed the improbable course amid flagwaving and foot-stomping, cheering, hugging and patriotic singing at the Olympic Field House.

The Americans defeated Finland, 4–2, and won the gold medal at the XIII Olympic Winter Games.

The victory followed by two days the most startling result in recent Olympic history—the 4–3 upset of the Soviet Union,—and touched off a nationwide celebration. The Russians later gained the silver medal with a 9–2 victory over Sweden, which captured the bronze medal.

Twenty years ago, in a less startling upset, the United States captured the gold in hockey at Squaw Valley, Calif. That triumphant team of 1960, however, did not evoke the national excitement that this young squad has. Not even the players themselves had expected to come this far. After all, they had never played together until last September, and were facing the national teams of other countries that had the advantage of years of training and experience. Yet, the Americans soared through the tournament undefeated, winning four games and tying one in the opening round, then upsetting the Russians before gaining the ultimate victory in a game that started at 11 A.M., and was televised live in the United States, including an 8 o'clock start in California.

"I'm sure the 20 guys can't believe it," said Mark Johnson, the center from the University of Wisconsin who scored the final goal of the three-goal comeback in the third period. "they'll probably wake up tomorrow morning and still won't believe it."

Small wonder, for in six of the seven games, the United States trailed at some point.

The fans believed it, though. Suddenly, the Olympic Field House rocked to the applause of the standing-room crowd, some of whom swarmed onto the blue-tinted ice and waved American flags, or hugged the red-white-and-blue-suited young Americans.

The Finns stood on the other side of the ice, patiently waiting for the cheering to stop so they could form the traditional reception line for handshaking that ends Olympic hockey games.

In contrast to the Soviet Olympic squad, which included seven players who had performed in the 1976 Games, and one who had been in the last three, only one American, Buzz Scheider, had appeared in the 1976 Olympics.

Schneider and the team captain, Mike Eruzione, are paid amateurs. They retained amateur status and Olympic eligiblity despite having played in semipro leagues because they had not signed professional contracts.

The Americans demonstrated that Brooks's style, which has come to be known as "American hockey," is more intuitive than the conventional style of the National Hockey League. The players employed more of the ice for passing, though they did have a larger rink with which to work. This rink was 100 feet wide, 15 feet wider than pro hockey rinks.

Along with faster movement and longer passes, the Americans also played the body—that is, they checked their opponents. Yet not one player was penalized for fighting in the Olympics.

Perhaps the constant body contact took its toll of the Finns as it did of the other American opponents and perhaps that is why the Americans were able to bounce back repeatedly in the third period. They did it against the Russians, after trailing by 3–2, and they did it again against the Finns. There are no overtimes in Olympic hockey.

The Finns, a collection of heady players whose style was based on using defense to create a favorable bounce of the puck, held a 2–1 edge going into the final period.

For the first time in these magic two weeks, some fans booed the Americans. The goaltender, Jim Craig, often flopped to the ice to snare bouncing pucks. For long stretches—in hockey, 30 seconds can be filled with dangerous shots—the Americans were unable to move.

The finale could have been disastrous for the United States. The Americans were called for three penalties and played short-handed for six of the final 20 minutes. Yet, they were the ones who pumped home three goals to a crescendo of applause.

At the game's end, President Carter was one of millions of Americans caught up with the latest American Dream in sports. More than 2,000 people sent telegrams, including such sports figures as Billy Martin and Terry Bradshaw. The fans at the arena included Vice President Mondale and Amy Carter.

In a phone call to Brooks following the game, the President said: "We were trying to do business and nobody could do it. We were watching the TV with one eye and Iran and the economy with the other."

Brooks then put Eruzione on the phone.

"Tell your whole team how much I love them, and we look forward to seeing the whole team tomorrow," said Mr. Carter. All of the United States Olympic athletes were to be guests at the White House the next morning.

Another 10,000 fans were in the arena for the awards ceremony after the game. They stood and applauded through the "Stars and Stripes Forever" while players, standing one behind the other, waved.

In a line next to them were the Russians, flanked by the Swedes.

Lord Killanin, president of the International Olympic Committee, took the first of 20 gold medals—although the team victory counts as only one—and put it around Craig's neck. Each of his teammates in turn stood on the highest of the three medal-winners platforms, bowing his head and beaming as the medal was hung. Then he would raise a fist to the crowd, bringing even louder cheers.

Eruzione, the captain, was last. Then the team snaked its way around the rink in a victory lap.

This crowd was not as festive as that assembled for the game with the Soviet Union. Perhaps the early Sunday morning start—after a late Olympic Saturday night—was the reason. In other games, players and fans fed off one another.

But in the final game the players were not as sharp. Their nervousness showed. "For the first time," explained Lou Vairo, one of Brooks's assistants, "we've got something to lose."

Indeed, no one had expected a victory over the Russians, a team that had averaged 10 goals against each of its other Olympic opponents and one that had beaten the American Olympians, 10–3, in a Madison Square Garden exhibition 72 hours before the Games began.

The Finns had lost two first-round games, and they, too, had nothing to lose. They played waiting hockey in the opening period, content to allow the gold lion on their jerseys to be the most intimidating part of their game.

After half a period, they finally made their move. Jukka Porvari stole the puck from Ken Morrow, a defenseman drafted by the New York Islanders, and drilled a 55-foot slap shot past Craig.

Early in the second period, seconds after Mike Ramsey scooted out of the penalty box, the Americans tied the score on Steve Christoff's shot. But within two minutes they trailed again when Schneider was sent off for slashing and Mikko Leinonen tallied a power-play goal. The United States' momentum was stalled.

In the last 20 minutes they reappeared as a team, though. On a two-on-one breakaway Dave Christian of Warroad, Minn., whose father had scored the winning goal in the 1960 game against the Russians, fed another Minnesotan, Phil Verchota, to tie the score.

61

And then the United States had its first lead of the game, with Johnson passing the disk from behind the net to Rob McClanahan, who stuffed it home.

With fewer than 14 minutes remaining, however, Neal Broten was penalized for hooking. In the next two minutes the short-handed Americans scrambled and somehow managed to halt the Finnish attack, with Craig making four saves in the stretch.

Six seconds after Broten returned, Christian was caught for tripping, and again the Finns had five skaters to four for the United States. This time the Americans yielded no shots. But within seven minutes Verchota was caught for roughing and went to the penalty box.

This time Johnson provided the crusher, scoring a short-handed goal for a 4–2 lead. Everyone left the bench to mob Johnson, except for Brooks, who looked at the clock and saw there were 3 minutes 35 seconds remaining.

There were no more goals, however, as Craig, who wound up stopping 91.57 percent of the shots fired at him in the seven games, protected the lead.

Then it was over, and Team America was only a memory.

"We came together six months ago," said a wistful Eruzione. "Different backgrounds, different ethnic beliefs. The saddest thing is that after this, after we see the President tomorrow, we'll go our different ways."

14: THE NATION CELEBRATES
LAKE PLACID . . .

Dave Anderson

When the buzzer sounded, they hugged each other and tossed their sticks and gloves up to the people who were chanting "U.S.A., U.S.A.," and danced with those who had skidded onto the ice with American flags large and small. Now, about half an hour after the victory over Finland had assured them of Olympic gold medals, the United States hockey team appeared in the Lake Placid High School auditorium in their red, white and blue uniforms, and, of course, shoes instead of skates. One by one, smiling and laughing with the euphoria of their triumph, they hurried up the steps to the small wooden stage and flopped into big black vinyl chairs to await their joyous inquisition. To the side, their coach, Herb Brooks, stood at a microphone.

"You're watching a group of people who startled the athletic world, not the hockey world, but the athletic world," the coach began. "These people are deserving because of their age and what they had to accomplish in a short time. As a father, you kick your children in the butt a lot but fathers and mothers love their children as I love this hockey team."

For six months, Herb Brooks had been kicking his players in the butt, screaming at them, snarling at them. Now it had all been worth it. Now they were the Olympic champions. Now they were America's team, having shocked the Soviet Union and themselves with a 4–3 victory Friday night and having rallied with three goals in the final period yesterday against Finland, just as the 1960 United States Olympic hockey team had rallied with six goals in the final period against Czechoslovakia for the gold medal at Squaw Valley, Calif.

"Is there one word," the players were asked now, "to describe what you've done?"

"Well," replied Mike Eruzione, the captain, "we're all a bunch of big doolies now."

To his listeners, doolies was a new word. Mike Eruzione turned back to where Phil Verchota, a blond left wing from Duluth, Minn., who had coined the word.

"I got a gold today, so I'm a big doolie," Phil Verchota explained. "It just means big wheel, big gun, bit shot."

"I have a question for Coach Brooks," a man called, prompting boos from the players. "Do you expect now to be appointed the coach of the U.S. national team?"

As the coach began to answer, several players yelled, "Gong, gong," and the coach grinned.

"If so," the coach was saying now, "the first thing I'll do is phone up all these athletes who are making a lot of money in the N.H.L. to fund us. But in a short time I'll be known as Herb Who?"

Suddenly another player appeared, Jack O'Callahan, holding a bottle of beer. He stumbled up the steps to the stage as his teammates cheered, then he exchanged the beer for some red wine.

"Jim Craig," someone asked the goaltender, "how do you describe the pressure of playing seven games in 13 days?"

"The six days of practice were the only things that bothered me, the seven games were fun," he said. "But first, I want to mention Steve Janaszak," he said, referring to the backup goaltender from St. Paul, Minn. "He's the only one of us who never got on the ice in the Olympic tournament, but he was a great influence on me and he busted his butt for us and I want to thank him publicly for making me a better person."

To the applause of his teammates, Steve Janaszak walked to Jim Craig and they embraced.

"Coach Brooks," another newsman called, "what did Vice President Mondale say after the game?"

"The first thing he said," Herb Brooks joked, "was that these people had to register for the draft Monday morning. But seriously, he told us that we don't have to prove our way of life is better through state-run sports, we can do it through amateur bodies."

By now Jack O'Callahan was sitting on the floor of the stage, leaning against a long table.

"As the only player from Charlestown, Mass.," called a Boston newsman, "what do you have to say?"

"Well," said the husky defenseman, standing up slowly, "Charlestown is in the shadow of Bunker Hill, and the Americans won at Bunker Hill, and the Americans won at Lake Placid."

Again the players cheered. Then somebody asked how all the midwestern players, mostly from Minnesota, had related to the Massachusetts players.

"We're 20 guys playing on the U.S. Olympic hockey team, we're not from Massachusetts or Minnesota," said Mike Eruzione, who is from Winthrop, Mass. "Out of that Olympic Village, that's all that matters, not whether we're from Minnesota or from Boston."

"But there are a lot of guys," added David Silk of Scituate, Mass., with a grin, "who wish they were from Boston."

At the side of the stage, Herb Brooks smiled.

"Is there," somebody asked now, "any favorite Brooksism to describe what happened here?"

"Well," said John Harrington, a right wing, quietly famous among his teammates for his imitations of the coach, "we were damned if we did and damned if we didn't. Fool me once, shame on you; fool me twice, shame on me. We reloaded, we went up to that tiger and spit in his eye. We went to the well again—the water was colder, the water was deeper. It's a good example of why we won the game. And for lack of a better phrase, that just about wraps it up."

His teammates were roaring now, and even Herb Brooks was smiling, sort of.

"Would you say," John Harrington was asked, "that Herb Brooks is a big doolie?"

"Sometimes he thinks he's a real big doolie," John Harrington said, smiling while peeking behind him at the coach. "But yeah, he's a real big doolie tonight."

"Jack O'Callahan," somebody called, "your history is bad, the Americans didn't win at Bunker Hill."

Still sitting on the stage, Jack O'Callahan was holding a bottle of champagne now.

"I don't want to hear that," the big defenseman replied firmly. "What do you think there's a monument there for? They won, they won."

But he knew who won the Olympic hockey gold medal. And so did everybody else all over the world.

. . . And in New York City
Dudley Clendinen

It was Jubilation Sunday.

At Radio City Music Hall, a capacity crowd of 6,000 parents and children rustled into quiet as a page, Steve Bridges, mounted the stage to bid them welcome to the 2 P.M. performance of the musical version of "Snow White and the Seven Dwarfs." It was a family crowd, come to watch a fairy tale.

And then Mr. Bridges gave them a piece of news: Five minutes earlier, the United States Olympic hockey team had beaten Finland, 4–2. The gold medal was America's.

"And the place just erupted," said Patricia Robert, the Music Hall spokesman.

The audience heaved, came cheering to its feet and began to sing "The Star-Spangled Banner." The orchestra joined in and, Mrs. Robert said, "we had two or three minutes of absolute joy, which I'm sure was reflected all over New York."

It was, and all over the nation, too. While it was Finland that the young American team had rallied to beat, it was a previous victory that first stirred the patriotic glee. Finland was the last test, yet still a surrogate for Friday's 4–3 upset of the Soviet Union. Sunday's game was the fulfillment of the ecstatic promise of Friday afternoon.

Hence the jubilation, which spread through America's homes and halls, barrooms and playing fields. It was, in a time of international tension and fatigue, as if the nation had been given a great present.

In the electric moments after the victory, a delighted President Carter telephoned the team in the dressing room from the White House. "Tell the whole team we're extremely proud of them," he told Coach Herb Brooks. "They played like true champions. We're so proud. We were trying to do business, and nobody could do it. We were watching TV with one eye and Iran and the economy with the other."

Vice President Mondale, who comes from Minnesota hockey country and admits to being "sort of" a hockey freak, was at the game. He jumped up with fists raised after each American goal, and said afterward, "This is one of the greatest moments I've been through in my life."

The general feeling of elation struck particularly in Minnesota, which is home to more than half the Olympic team. People honked at one another on Minnesota highways. Patrons in taverns and restaurants cheered wildly at any mention of the Olympics or hockey.

After all, the University of Minnesota won the National Collegiate hockey championship last season under Coach Herb Brooks, and now another team headed by Brooks and packed with athletes from the Gopher State had overcome the Soviet Union, Finland and the rest of the world to capture the gold medal.

Jack Poulsen, president of the National Fly the Flag Crusade, with headquarters in Minneapolis, said that as soon as the game had ended he jumped into his station wagon, which was covered with 75 American flags, and started driving around town. "I was driving around tooting my horn for America," he said. "How can you not be happy on a day like this?"

Many residents in Eveleth, Minn., the hometown of Mark Pavelich, a member of the American squad, gathered at the Elks Club to watch the game on television. Among them was Pat Bastianelli, a city councilman.

"Just super, just super," he said. "Here's a bunch of kids that northern Minnesota can be proud of. No, the state, the country, the world can be proud of them."

Minutes after the victory, the small town of Winthrop, Mass., home of Mike Eruzione, the team captain, erupted with a blaring of horns from a motorcade of several dozen cars, led by a flatbed truck crammed with young people waving American flags and shouting, "We're No. 1!"

Many of the town's residents gathered in front of the modest Eruzione home, where family members and friends stood on the second-story front porch spraying champagne and beer on one another and on cheering neighbors.

Eruzione's sister, Jeanie, 28, said the wife of Massachusetts Gov. Edward J. King, who is also a resident of Winthrop, a coastal community abutting the northern edge of Boston, phoned to voice her congratulations. But for the family, a major highlight was watching Eruzione during his phone conversation with President Carter after the game.

"I could tell by the look on his face that he was thinking, 'Oh wow, I don't believe I'm talking to the President,'" said his sister.

In Kansas City, Mo., a crowd of 14,546 at a National Basketball Association game interrupted the nationally televised contest between the Kings and the

Milwaukee Bucks and sang the national anthem a second time. Three players—Phil Ford and Ernie Grunfeld of the Kings, and Quinn Buckner of the Bucks—were on the gold-medal basketball team at Montreal in 1976. They knew the feeling.

"It was so big it got the whole country interested," said Buckner of the hockey team's effort. "It's a very good feeling. I know what it's like to be the underdog and come out on top."

Some fans suffered a disappointment. About a dozen in Memphis, Tenn., demonstrated at the local ABC-TV affiliate after station officials decided to show a church service rather than the hockey game. The officials said they had made a previous commitment to carry the church program. A man who owned a helicopter was so angry that he flew over the city for an hour trailing a 100-foot banner that read: "WHBQ— What Happened to Our Hockey Game?"

At a concrete rink next to the United Nations in New York City, the happy news came while the Nationals and the Maple Leafs, roller-hockey teams in the East End Hockey Association, were playing their regular Sunday afternoon game. Every so often, John Caulfield, a 27-year-old Hunter College student who organizes the games, yelled to a little boy watching from the sidelines: "Hey, Eddy, run home and see what's happening at the Olympics!" On his third run back from the television set at home, Eddy brought the news of the victory.

"This really shows the Americans were more aggressive and wanted the gold medal more," said Jon Vercesi, a player with the Maple Leafs. "It really makes you feel very patriotic, the whole Olympics. The players are amateurs, and when you see how hard they work and how happy they are, you really feel like you wish it were you." Mr. Caulfield listened and said: "I don't think anyone is happy about Russian foreign policy right now, and there's a feeling there's not a lot we can do, except pass resolutions at the U.N. and beat the Russians at the Olympics."

And cheer, which people all over the city interrupted themselves to do when they saw or heard of the victory. They cheered over Bloody Marys and brunch at the Red Blazer restaurant on the Upper East Side, and they cheered in Avery Fisher Hall at Lincoln Center, when the violinist Alexander Schneider told the audience that had come to hear him perform with the Brandenburg Ensemble, "We beat the Finns, 4 to 2."

"I guess this is sort of a fairy tale, too," said Mrs. Robert from her office at the Music Hall, where the fairy tale about Snow White was under way.

★★★★★★★★★★★★★★★★★★★★★★★★★

EPILOGUE: AT THE WHITE HOUSE . . .

★★★★★★★★★★★★★★★★★★★★★★★★★

Steven R. Weisman

Before a flag-waving, squealing crowd at the White House the day after the Olympics ended, President Carter embraced the United States' Winter Olympic athletes as "modern-day American heroes."

But shortly thereafter, there was talk of Eric Heiden presenting a petition from the athletes opposing the President's call for a boycott of the Games in Moscow next July.

"I hope we don't boycott," the speed skating star told reporters during a festive luncheon in the East Room of the White House, attended by scores of athletes in their red, white and blue warm-up suits. "The winter athletes in general just don't feel a boycott is the right thing."

Earlier the President reiterated his stand on the boycott in his opening remarks at the ceremony, while expressing sympathy for athletes because of the setback that a withdrawal from the Games would impose.

"To go through all of that personal sacrifice is indeed a great achievement," the President said. "And then to suffer an injury or some other obstacle that eliminates you from final competition is tough to accept. But to go through that sacrifice and then have your chances dashed by something that really has nothing to do with your own efforts can be an even harder blow." The President then pledged to meet in the near future with "a representative group of our summer athletes" to try to set up "an alternative world-class competition for them this summer that does not harm Olympic principles and will not harm future Olympic Games."

Mr. Carter's remarks provided the only sobering note in a day of rippling excitement among the usually blasé White House staff, which turned out by the hundreds to cheer the arrival of the athletes as the United States Marine Band blared the Olympic theme.

The crowd of staff members and visitors, gathered on the South Lawn, waved tiny American flags and whooped with delight as the medal winners marched, one by one, up the stairs to the south portico to be greeted, kissed and embraced by a beaming President. They were also welcomed at the top of the stairs by Rosalynn Carter and Joan Mondale, wife of the Vice President.

Heiden bounded up the stairs, waving an American flag and wearing his warmup suit, his favorite red, yellow and blue knitted cap and all five gold medals. He and the President embraced.

In the evening, the President drew enthusiastic applause when he once again spoke for withdrawal from the Games, in a talk before 1,000 members of the Order of Ahepa, the American Hellenic Educational Progress Association. "Wouldn't it be wonderful," Mr. Carter told the crowd of Greek-Americans, gathered at the Washington Sheraton Hotel, "if we had a permanent Summer Olympic site in Greece?"—a renewal of a suggestion that the President has made to the Olympic community before.

The hockey team loped up the steps of the White House in windbreakers, sheepskin jackets and cowboy hats, many of them also waving flags.

"The U.S. hockey team!" Mr. Carter exclaimed at the ceremony. "Their victory was one of the most breathtaking upsets, not only in Olympic history but in the entire history of sports."

He also embraced and kissed Linda Fratianne and Leah Mueller, who won silver medals in figure skating and speed skating, respectively, and Beth Heiden, Eric's sister, winner of a bronze medal in speed skating.

"For me, as President of the United States of America, this is one of the proudest moments that I have ever experienced," Mr. Carter declared.

Mr. Carter made a few jokes, one about the transportation problems at Lake Placid, N.Y. He said that after he had invited Mr. Brooks and the hockey team to the White House, Mr. Brooks told him that some buses would be available at Lake Placid to bring them.

"I said, 'If you don't mind, Herb, I think I'll send a couple of planes to pick you up,' " the President told the crowd. "So here they are, and we're very proud of them. You have conducted yourselves in the finest traditions of our country and of the Olympic ideal. You have thrilled the entire world."

. . . And at Lake Placid
Dave Anderson

In retrospect, he was an omen. One day more than two weeks ago, before the XIII Olympic Winter Games, the afternoon sun glistened off the frozen Ausable River between steep forests of white birch at Lake Placid. Below, in long black pants and a gray sweater, a teenager with a hockey stick skated along the endless ice. Every so often he would retrieve his puck, shoot it and skate after it again, so alone and yet so content.

Now, with the Olympics over the most dominant memory here is that of the United States hockey players, who stirred the nation by winning the gold medal.

Like that lonely teenager, many of them learned to skate and shoot on frozen rivers and frozen lakes, in Minnesota and Massachusetts, and now they are America's team, the conqueror of the Soviet Union's renowned squad, which embarrassed the National Hockey League all-stars in the Challenge Cup a year ago at Madison Square Garden. The nation marveled as Eric Heiden swept the five men's gold medals in speed skating, but it suffered with the hockey team's climb to the gold-medal pedestal. As long as your team wins, suffering is always more fun.

But the glory of America's triumphs here was a reminder of the grandeur of the Olympics, when the athletes are at center stage instead of the politicians.

By acting as host to the entire United States Olympic team at the White House yesterday, President Carter appears to be contradicting himself on the value of Olympic participation and triumphs. At a luncheon, he thanked some Olympians for competing at Lake Placid. But he also reaffirmed his intention to prevent other Olympians from competing at Moscow this summer because of the Soviet intervention in Afghanistan. Morally the Olympic boycott remains correct, but the success of the hockey team and Eric Heiden at Lake Placid will prompt sympathy for the worldwide significance of similar American triumphs at Moscow.

During the Olympic fortnight, a Yugoslav official was asked if his nation intended to go to Moscow, and he replied, "Yes, yes, we will go, but without the Americans it will not be the Olympics." That is precisely the point. Without the United States and without whatever other nations join the boycott, it will not be the Olympics, it will be the non-Olympics, an embarrassment to the Soviet Union, which hoped to use the Games as a showcase.

As always, there are memories of moments that never appeared on television, that were never worth a headline or even a paragraph at the time. The strange, hooflike sound of leather mittens being pounded as Eric Heiden swooped around the last turn on the speed skating oval that dominated the village panorama. The sudden speed of the downhill racers flashing under spectators floating in a chairlift above the Whiteface Mountain course. And, of course, the hockey moments.

In one, Herb Brooks, the United States coach, was talking about his team of collegians and castoffs.

"It's a long, hard week," he said. "If we win the gold, we're going to have to do it with the intangibles."

74

In another, someone is asking the hockey players how many intend to grow a beard now that the Olympic tournament is over, and a voice squeaks, "How many of us *can* grow one?" And in another, Bob Cleary, a member of the 1960 United States hockey team, which won the gold medal, is talking about how Jack Reiley, the coach of that team, asked the United States Olympic Committee to bring back all the players for a reunion here, but how the Olympic committee rejected the idea.

The next time the Winter Olympics is in the United States, perhaps in the year 2000, maybe the Olympic committee will remember to reunite America's team from 1980.

But perhaps this was the last Olympics as we know them; perhaps they will never be quite the same again. If the United States' boycott of Moscow materializes, the Soviet Union is likely to discover a reason to boycott Los Angeles for the Summer Games there in 1984.

In between, the 1984 Winter Games are scheduled for Sarajevo, Yugoslavia, the site of the assassination in 1914 of Archduke Francis Ferdinand, heir to the Austrian throne, which ignited World War I.

By 1984, who knows what the political climate in Yugoslavia will be? But in Sarajevo's advance brochures, the Olympic organizers there are already promising prompt bus service, just as the Lake Placid organizers did.

As unfortunate and unforgivable as the bus hassle was for thousands of spectators here, it should be recorded that just about everything else was handled efficiently by pleasant people. And the one true moment of shame is on the conscience of the International Olympic Committee, not the local organizers. Outside the Prague Inn nearly two weeks ago, an "Olympic Rentals Available" sign was up as the Taiwan Olympic team, having lost its legal battle with the international committee in the State Court of Appeals, gathered in the chill on the afternoon of the opening ceremony. For the members of the Taiwan delegation, it was their closing ceremony. They were about to depart.

But in all the souvenir shops on Main Street throughout the XIII Olympic Winter Games, the words on the back of many Olympic pins were "Made in Taiwan."

But the most last memory of the 1980 Winter Olympics has to be of the 20 young men, and their coach. Because they beat the team that was supposed to be unbeatable, the team that had been unbeatable for so many years.

And because the timing was so perfect for a miracle on ice.

GAME HIGHLIGHTS

Game One

Feb. 12

Sweden	1	0	1—2
United States	0	1	1—2

First Period

Sture Andersson scored the only goal of the period, at 11 minutes 4 seconds. Lars Molin and Per Lundquist assisted. There was one penalty, to Mike Ramsey of the United States at 13:34.

Second Period

The United States tied the game on Dave Silk's goal at 19:32, with Ramsey and Mark Johnson assisting. The only penalty was to Mats Waltin of Sweden at 5:20.

Third Period

Sweden went ahead by 2–1 on Thomas Eriksson's goal at 4:45, with Molin and Lundquist again assisting. The United States then tied the score with 27 seconds remaining in the game on Bill Baker's goal. Mark Pavelich and Buzz Schneider assisted. The penalties in the period were to Tomas Jonsson of Sweden (5:32), Eriksson (7:45 and 12:17), Mike Eruzione of the United States (7:45) and Ken Morrow of the United States (14:15).

Sweden had 36 shots on goal for the game (16 in the first period, 11 in the second and 9 in the third). The United States had 29 shots on goal (7, 12 and 10).

The goaltenders were Pelle Lindbergh for Sweden

and Jim Craig for the United States. The attendance was 4,000.

Game Two

Feb. 14

United States	2	2	3—7
Czechosolovakia	2	0	1—3

First Period

Czechoslovakia scored first on a goal by Jaroslav Pouzar, at 2 minutes 23 seconds. He was assisted by Frantisek Kaberle and Milan Novy. The United States scored at 4:39 of the period, with Mike Eruzione getting the goal and Neal Broten assisting. The United States went ahead by 2–1 on Mark Pavelich's goal at 5:45. Buzz Schneider and John Harrington assisted. Czechoslovakia again tied the score at 2–2 at 12:07 on Marian Stastny's goal. Stastny's brother Peter got an assist.

The penalties in the period were to Phil Verchota of the United States (at 12:20), Milan Chalupa of Czechoslovakia (14:51) and Anton Stastny of Czechoslovakia (18:29).

Second Period

The United States scored twice to go ahead by 4–2. Schneider, with Pavelich assisting, scored at 4:33, and Mark Johnson, on an assist by Rob McClanahan, scored at 15:28. The penalties in the period were to McClanahan (6:17), Pouzar (10:55), and Dave Christian of the United States (10:55).

Third Period

Verchota's goal at 2:59 gave the United States a 5–2 lead, Christian assisting. The United States got its sixth goal at 3:59, with Schneider scoring his second goal and Harrington assisting. The score was 6–3 after

Jiri Novak of Czechoslovakia scored at 5:36, on an assist by Vincenc Lukac. McClanahan then closed the scoring at 10:54, Johnson assisting. The penalties in the period were to Steve Christoff of the United States and Stastny of Czechoslovakia (double minors) at 16:55).

The United States had 27 shots on goal for the game, 11 in the first period, 5 in the second and 11 in the third. Czechoslovakia had 31 shots on goal (13, 6, and 12).

The goaltenders were Jim Craig for the United States and Jiri Kralik for Czechoslovakia. The attendance was 7,125.

Game Three

Feb. 16

Norway	1	0	0—1
United States	0	3	2—5

First Period

Geir Myhre of Norway scored the only goal of the period, at 4 minutes 19 seconds. The penalties in the period were to Rune Molberg of Norway (1:21 and 3:56), Mark Johnson of the United States (2:38), Phil Verchota of the United States (4:39), Pederson of Norway (5:37) and Buzz Schneider of the United States (14:01).

Second Period

The United States tied the game at 1–1 on Mike Eruzione's unassisted goal at 41 seconds. Johnson scored at 4:51, assisted by Rob McClanahan and Dave Christian. Dave Silk's goal at 13:31, assisted by Mark Pavelich and Ken Morrow, gave the United States a 3–1 advantage. The penalties in the period were to Knut Andresen of Norway (0:25 and 10:21), Nilsen of Norway (15:44) and Eric Strobel of the United States (15:44).

Third Period

Mark Wells of the United States scored at 4:28, with Silk and Verchota getting assists. The final United States goal was by Morrow at 11:29, with assists by McClanahan and Strobel. The penalties in the period were to Pederson of Norway (1:55), Bill Baker of the United States (5:03), Myhre of Norway (a double minor at 19:36), Bob Suter of the United States (double minor at 19:36), and Baker of the United States (19:54).

Norway had 22 shots on goal (9, 7 and 6), while the United States had 43 shots on goal (16, 16 and 11).

The goaltenders were Jim Marthinsen for Norway and Jim Craig for the United States. The attendance was 1.400.

Game Four

Feb. 18

United States 2	2	3—7
Rumania 0	1	1—2

First Period

Buzz Schneider opened the scoring for the United States at 12 minutes 3 seconds, with assists by Mark Pavelich and John Harrington. Eric Strobel of the United States, with assists by Schneider and Mike Ramsey, followed with a goal at 15:52. The only penalty of the period was to Traian Cazacu of Rumania, at 3:58.

Second Period

The United States took a 3–0 lead on a goal by Mark Wells at 9:34. Phil Verchota and Ken Morrow assisted. Doru Tureanu scored for Rumania at 13:40, assisted by Constantin Nistor. Schneider then got his second goal of the game at 17:05, with an assist by

John Harrington. The penalties in the period were to Mike Ramsey of the United States (at 0:47), Pavelich (12:59) and Ion Berdila of Rumania (19:55).

Third Period

Steve Christoff of the United States scored at 8:14, assisted by Jack O'Callahan. Alexandru Halauga scored for Rumania's at 12:48, with an assist by Doru Iosif Morosan. Then Neal Broten's goal at 16:12 gave the United States a 6–2 lead. Mike Eruzione assisted on the play. Rob McClanahan, with an assist by Mark Johnson, closed the United States scoring with a goal at 18:09. The penalties in the period were to Sandor Gali of Rumania (2:18), Laszlo Solyom of Rumania (6:46), Traian Cazacu of Rumania (19:03) and Johnson of the United States (19:03).

The United States had 51 shots on goal for the game (20 in the first period, 16 in the second and 15 in the third), while Rumania had 21 shots on goal (9, 9 and 3).

The goaltenders were Jim Craig for the United States and Valerian Netedu and Gheorshe Hutan for Rumania. The attendance was 8,500.

Game Five

Feb. 20

West Germany	2	0	0—2
United States	0	2	2—4

First Period

West Germany took a 2–0 lead on an unassisted goal by Horst-Peter Kretschmer at 1 minute 50 seconds and a goal by Udd Aiessling, assisted by Ernst Hofner and Kretschmer, at 19:45. The penalties in the period were to Peter Scharf of West Germany (at 4:55), Jack O'Callahan of the United States (13:11), Hans Zach of West Germany (19:41), Dave Christian of the United States (19:41) and Mark Johnson of the United States (19:41).

Second Period

Rob McClanahan scored on a breakaway for the United States at 7:40, Johnson and Christian assisting. Neal Broten of the United States then tied the game with a goal at 18:31. Eric Strobel and Mike Eruzione got assists. The penalties in the period were to Rainer Philipp of West Germany (6:26), Bob Suter of the United States (6:26) and Mike Ramsey of the United States (12:55).

Third Period

The United States went ahead on McClanahan's second goal of the game, at 1:17, with Johnson and Christian again assisting. Phil Verchota got the final United States goal at 4:17, with assists going to Christian and Mark Wells. The penalties in the period were to Verchota (7:19). Steve Christoff of the United States (13:45), Ken Morrow of the United States (15:10) and Kretschmer of West Germany (19:12).

West Germany had 26 shots on goal for the game (7 in the first period, 6 in the second and 13 in the third). The United States had 32 shots on goal (14, 9 and 9).

The goaltenders were Sigmund Suttner for West Germany and Jim Craig for the United States.

Game Six

Feb. 22

United States	2	0	2—4
Soviet Union	2	1	0—3

First Period

Vladimir Krutov of the Soviet Union opened the scoring with a goal at 9 minutes 12 seconds. Aleksei

Kasatonov assisting. Buzz Schneider, assisted by Mark Pavelich, scored for the United States at 14:03. The Soviet Union went ahead by 2–1 on Sergei Makarov's goal at 17:34, with Vladimir Golikov assisting. Then with one second remaining in the period, Mark Johnson of the United States scored to tie the game. Dave Christian and Dave Silk got assists. The only penalty of the period was to Boris Mikhailov of the Soviet Union, at 3:25.

Second Period

The Soviet Union went ahead by 3–2 at 2:18 on a goal by Aleksandr Maltsev, with Krutov assisting. The penalties in the period were to John Harrington (0:58), Jim Craig of the United States (9:50), Yuri Lebedev of the Soviet Union (17:08) and Ken Morrow of the United States (17:08).

Third Period

The United States tied the score on Johnson's second goal of the game, at 8:39, with Silk again assisting. Mike Eruzione then scored the decisive goal for the United States at 10:00, with assists by Mark Pavelich and Harrington. The single penalty of the period was to Krutov, at 16:47.

The United States had 16 shots on goal for the game (8 in the first period, 2 in the second and 6 in the third). The Soviet Union had 39 shots on goal (18, 12 and 9).

The goaltenders were Jim Craig for the United States and Vladislav Tretyak and Vladimir Myshkin for the Soviet Union. The attendance was 10,000.

Game Seven

Feb. 24

United States 0	1	3—4
Finland 1	1	0—2

First Period

Jukka Porvari of Finland opened the scoring with a goal in 9 minutes 20 seconds. Mikko Leinonen and Lasse Litma assisted. The one penalty of the period was to Koskinen (at 4:54).

Second Period

Dave Christoff of United States tied the score at 1–1 with an unassisted goal at 4:39. Finland then regained the lead on Mikko Leinonen's goal at 6:30, with Hannu Haapalainen and Markku Kiimalainen assisting. The penalties in the period were to Mike Ramsey of the United States (2:37), Buzz Schneider of the United States (6:00) and Seppo Suoraniemi of Finland (15:52).

Third Period

The United States tied the score at 2–2 on Phil Verchota's goal at 2:25. Dave Christian got the assist. Rob McClanahan's goal at 6:05, with Johnson and Christian assisting, gave the United States a 3–2 advantage. Johnson closed out the United States scoring with a goal at 16:25. Christian got another assist. The penalties in the period were to Neal Broten of the United States (6:48), Christian (8:54) and Verchota (15:45).

The United States had 29 shots on goal for the game (14 in the first period, 8 in the second and 7 in the third). Finland had 23 shots on goal (7, 6 and 10).

The goaltenders were Jim Craig for the United States and Jorma Valtonen for Finland. The attendance was 10,000.

OLYMPIC HOCKEY STANDINGS

FINAL STANDINGS

MEDAL ROUND

	W	L	T	Pts	GF	GA
United States	2	0	1	5	10	7
Soviet Union	2	1	0	4	16	8
Sweden	0	1	2	2	7	14
Finland	0	2	1	1	7	11

Note: To complete the round robin, these standings include the U.S.-Sweden and Soviet Union-Finland games, which are also included in the division standings below.

DIVISION STANDINGS

RED DIVISION

	W	L	T	Pts	GF	GA
Soviet Union	5	0	0	10	51	11
Finland	3	2	0	6	26	18
Canada	3	2	0	6	28	12
Poland	2	3	0	4	15	23
Netherlands	1	3	1	3	16	43
Japan	0	4	1	1	7	36

BLUE DIVISION

	W	L	T	Pts	GF	GA
Sweden	4	0	1	9	26	7
United States	4	0	1	9	25	10
Czechoslovakia	3	2	0	6	34	15
Rumania	1	3	1	3	13	29
West Germany	1	4	0	2	21	30
Norway	0	4	1	1	9	36

★★★★★★★★ ★★★★★★★★★★★★★★
THE ROSTER
★★★★★★★★ ★★★★★★★★★★★★★★★

Bill Baker

The 6 foot, 1 inch, 195 pound defenseman from Grand
Rapids, Mich., scored the tying goal in the third period in
first game against Sweden. The 23-year-old was captain
of the University of Minnesota team, which won the National Collegiate championship last year.

Neal Broten

The 5-9, 155-pound, forward from Roseau, Minn., scored
a goal and had an assist in the Olympics. The 20-year-old
played one season for the University of Minnesota, where,
as a freshman, he established a school record for assists,
with 55. He was drafted on the second round by the Minnesota North Stars in 1979.

Dave Christian

The United States center from Warroad, Minn., led the
team in assists. The 5-11, 170-pounder played two seasons
for the University of North Dakota. He is a member of the
Christian family that has now won three Olympic gold
medals and a silver medal. The 21-year-old is the son of
Bill Christian, who played on the 1960 gold-medal team
and scored the winning goal in the United States' 3-2 victory over the Soviet Union; and the nephew of Roger
Christian, who played on 1960 and 1964 teams, and Gor-
don Christian, who played on the silver-medal winning
team of 1956.

Steve Christoff

A 6-1, 180-pounder from Richfield, Minn., scored the
team's first goal in the second period in game against
Finland. At 22 he has played three seasons at the University of Minnesota, scoring 77 goals and collecting 82 assists.

Jim Craig

This 22-year-old goalie from North Easton, Mass., was
perhaps the key to the United States's gold-medal victory.

The 6-1, 190-pounder played every minute of every game and allowed only 15 goals in seven games. He proved to be toughest in the third period when, three times, the United States had to come from behind to tie or win. He gave up only three last-period goals. He led Boston University to a collegiate championship in 1978 and has been drafted by the Atlanta Flames.

Mike Eruzione

The 5-10, 185-pound captain of the Olympic team, from Winthrop, Mass. This 25-year-old forward scored the winning goal in the 4-3 victory over the Soviet Union and a goal against Czechoslovakia. A graduate of Boston University, he played two seasons for Toledo in the International Hockey League as an amateur because he had not been drafted by a professional team.

John Harrington

This 22-year-old forward from Virginia, Minn., had two assists against Czechoslovakia and one against the Soviet Union. The 5-10, 180-pounder scored 65 goals in four seasons for the University of Minnesota at Duluth.

Steve Janaszak

This 5-8, 160-pound goalie from White Bear Lake, Minn., was the only American who did not play at Lake Placid. The 23-year-old was goaltender for the University of Minnesota's national championship team last season.

Mark Johnson

The 22-year-old center from Madison, Wis., played brilliantly in the Olympics, scoring five goals—two against the Soviet Union—and getting two assists. He was an all-American at the University of Wisconsin and college player of the year in 1979. The 5-9, 160-pounder is expected to sign with the Pittsburgh Penguins.

Rob McClanahan

This 5-10, 180-pound center from St. Paul, Minn., will be remembered for scoring the winning goal in the third period against Finland. He also had two goals against West Germany. The 22-year-old has one year of eligibility remaining at the University of Minnesota and was drafted by the Buffalo Sabres in 1978.

Ken Morrow

This 6-4, 210-pound defenseman, from Davison, Mich., was a reliable defender throughout the Olympics. The 23-year-old scored two goals and had one assist. He played for Bowling Green and was drafted in fourth round by the Islanders in 1976.

Jack O'Callahan

This 22-year-old defenseman from Charlestown, Mass., missed the first game against Sweden, but later had an assist against Rumania. The 6-1, 185-pounder was an all-American at Boston University last season and was drafted on the sixth round by Chicago Black Hawks in 1977.

Mark Pavelich

The 5-7, 160-pound center from Eveleth, Minn., had two assists against the Soviet Union. The 21-year-old was an All-American at the University of Minnesota at Duluth last season and is expected to return to school.

Mike Ramsey

A 6-3, 190-pound defenseman from Minneapolis, Ramsey played for the University of Minnesota. Last year the 19-year-old was drafted by Buffalo, becoming the first American to be selected in the first round. He is expected to join the Sabres this season.

Buzz Schneider

At 25 Schneider, from Babbitt, Minn., and the University of Minnesota is the oldest man on the American team. The 5-11, 184-pounder tied for the scoring lead with Johnson. He had four goals and three assists. He has played on four national teams, and was the only player on the team who played in the 1976 Games. Like Eruzione, he played in the minor leagues for two seasons as an amateur and has not been drafted.

Dave Silk

This 5-11, 190-pound forward from Scituate, Mass., scored two goals for the United States. The 22-year-old played for Boston University and was member of 1978 collegiate champions. He was drafted in fourth round by the Rangers in 1978.

Eric Strobel

This 21-year-old from Rochester, Minn., scored a goal against Rumania and collected an assist against West Germany and Norway. The 5-10, 175-pound forward played three seasons for the University of Minnesota, scoring 52 goals, and has one season of eligibility remaining. Be was drafted in the eighth round by Buffalo in 1978.

Bob Suter

The 5-9, 178-pound defenseman, from Madison, Wis,. had no points in the Olympics, but played superb defense. The 22-year-old was a member of the University of Wisconsin team that won the 1977 college championship.

Phil Verchota

The 23-year-old forward from Duluth, Minn., scored the tying goal against Finland and also scored against West Germany and Czechoslovakia. The 6-2, 195-pounder played for the University of Minnesota and was the fifth-round choice of the North Stars in 1976.

Mark Wells

This 5-9, 175-pound center from St. Clair Shores, Mich., had limited playing time in the Olympics. In four years at Bowling Green, the 22-year-old scored 77 goals and had 155 assists.